# KAFR EL-ELOW

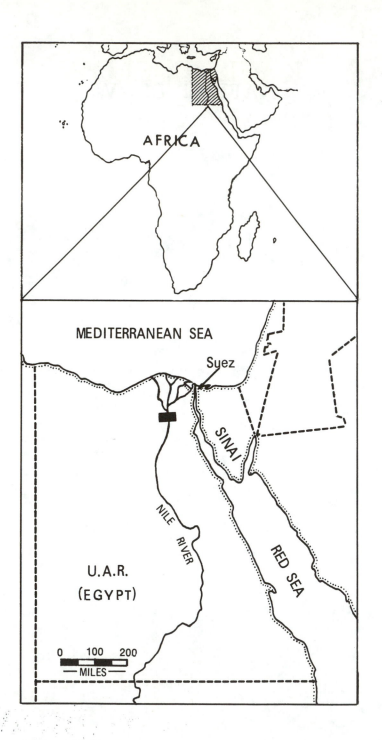

AFRICA

MEDITERRANEAN SEA

Suez

SINAI

NILE RIVER

U.A.R.
(EGYPT)

RED SEA

0    100    200
— MILES —

# KAFR EL-ELOW

## Continuity and Change in an Egyptian Community

### Second Edition

By

HANI FAKHOURI

*University of Michigan, Flint*

WAVELAND PRESS, INC.

Prospect Heights, Illinois

For information about this book, write or call:

Waveland Press, Inc.
P.O. Box 400
Prospect Heights, Illinois 60070
(312) 634-0081

**Cover photograph:** Vertical housing expansion in the old site of Kafr el-Elow.

Printed in the United States of America

7   6   5   4   3   2

# Foreword

## About the Author

Hani Fakhouri is presently a Professor of Anthropology and Sociology at the University of Michigan. He obtained a Ph.D. in Anthropology from Michigan State University. While at the University of Dayton and the University of Michigan, Dr. Fakhouri distinguished himself by winning several outstanding awards for excellence in teaching and scholarly research activities. Also, he was the recipient of the Visiting Professor of the Year Research Award in 1978 from the American Research Center in Egypt. In December 1985, Dr. Fakhouri was awarded a Fulbright Research Fellowship to continue his research activities in Egypt.

His field work in Egypt resulted in several articles for professional journals as well as this book. Dr. Fakhouri has pursued ethnographic field research in Jordan and Iraq. He is currently engaged in research focused upon tribal law and the settlement of disputes in the Middle East, and the study of continuity and change in Arab society.

## About the Book

Kafr el-Elow, the village described in this study, is eighteen miles south of Cairo, situated in the midst of one of the most densely populated areas in the world. It is now undergoing rapid industrialization and urbanization. It is an area with a long history, due to the fact that the Egyptian civilization was highly developed there by 2500 B.C. As the old ways continue and the new spring up beside them this area has become one of sharp contrasts in almost every dimension of life. These contrasts and changes are a constant theme of the case study, which describes the economy, family and kinship system, religion, government, and education. The author, however, always remains mindful of his obligations to provide basic information on the traditional culture and social system. The case study ends with a chapter devoted explicitly to an analysis of cultural change in which the author grapples with some basic problems relevant to all changing folk communities.

Kafr el-Elow, is significant because it is an industrial, urban village that has a traditional folk-peasant cultural base. It is, therefore, a type of community that is widespread in the world today, particularly in developing countries. It is also of special interest to us because it is located in the Middle East, a part of the world where severe tensions, which will probably continue for some time, have developed. Behind the news of international conflicts there are the folk living in small communities and struggling with life and with changes in the conditions of their existence. It is at this level that the meaning of revolution as well as technological change can become clear. The 1952 revolution in Egypt and its consequences can be seen in a very different perspective than that afforded by most of the news media or governing agencies in the United States. The primary task of anthropology is to attempt to understand the folk and the conditions governing how they live.

Hani Fakhouri, in his research and interpretations, had the special advantage of having been reared in Jordan and thus being intimately familiar with the general cultural type represented by this Egyptian village. His personal and subjective grasp of the situation is tempered and extended by the use of objective research methods, including questionnaires, surveys, and basic census data.

GEORGE AND LOUISE SPINDLER

# Preface

My initial research in Kafr el-Elow was carried out between November 1964 and May 1966 under the auspices of the Social Research Center at the American University in Cairo, Egypt. After the original manuscript was finished, I returned to Kafr el-Elow during the summer of 1968, this time under the terms of a grant from the Research Center at the University of Dayton, Ohio. A former research assistant and I talked to my original informants and to village leaders to ascertain what changes had occurred during the two-year period, 1966–1968. It was obvious that the physical appearance of the village had changed considerably. More homes had been constructed, and a new and larger mosque had been built to replace the old one and to accommodate the continually increasing population in the village due to the flow of migrant workers from various parts of Egypt. Moreover, the main streets and roads had been paved and officially named, reflecting the names of the various clans in the village. Expansion in the industrial sector was also noticeable. In this study, I have described Kafr el-Elow as it appeared to me between 1966 and 1968, which is reflected in the first seven chapters of this book. In December 1985, I returned to Kafr el-Elow as a Fulbright Research Fellow to examine and analyze the continuity and change which has been occurring in the community during the past two decades. The result of the second phase of this study is reflected in Chapter Eight of this book.

To Dr. Laila Shukry el-Hamamsy and Dr. Saad Gadalla, Director and Assistant Director, respectively, of the Social Research Center, I wish to express special gratitude. Others at the Social Research Center to whom I owe special thanks are my field assistants, Mr. Mohammad Fikri, Miss Fadwa el Guindi, and Miss Zeinab Gamal Hassan, the latter two for collecting valuable information about the women of Kafr el-Elow which, in this culture, only female investigators could secure, and to the entire staff of the center for their kind assistance. All contributed in no small measure to the completion of this study.

The following members of the Anthropology Department at Michigan State University gave friendly guidance and helpful criticism: Dr. Iwao Ishino, Chairman of the department, Dr. Elizabeth Bacon, and Dr. Leonard Kasdan.

Acknowledgment of indebtedness is likewise due my generous and kind colleague, Dr. Mary Jo Huth of the Sociology–Anthropology Department at the University of Dayton, who read the entire manuscript and who offered extremely helpful suggestions in regard to literary style.

Last, but not least, I wish to acknowledge the people of Kafr el-Elow, with whom I shared fifteen months of my life, for whose boundless courtesy, hospitality, goodwill, and generous assistance I will always be grateful.

HANI FAKHOURI

# Contents

Foreword                                                          v

Preface                                                         vii

Introduction                                                      1

1. The Community                                                  5
   *Geographical Setting—Physical Description of Kafr el-
   Elow—Historical Setting—Population—Health—Housing—
   Clothing—Diet—Public Utilities and Services*

2. The Village Economy                                           27
   *Agriculture—Industry—Commerce and Other Sources of
   Income—Types of Occupations and Commercial Activities
   in Kafr el-Elow*

3. Family and Kinship Organization                               55
   *Family Structure in Kafr el-Elow—Kinship Terminology—
   Kinship Roles—The Mate Selection Process—Pre-Nuptial
   Rituals—The Wedding Day* (Youm Iddukhla)*—Polygyny—
   Widowhood—Divorce—Social Class*

4. Religious Beliefs and Practices                               75
   *The Basic Tenets of Islam—Islam's Impact on the Villagers—
   Universal Islamic Practices—Practices Associated with Islam
   in Kafr el-Elow*

5. Education: Formal and Informal                                96
   *Traditional Education—Modern Education—Education be-
   yond the Elementary Level—Formal Education of Females—
   The Impact of Formal Education on the Villagers—The
   Mass Media*

6. Village Government                                           105
   *The Traditional Government—The Modern Government—
   The New Political Horizon—The Settlement of Disputes*

7. Summary and Conclusions      116

*The Community of Kafr el-Elow in Retrospect — Change in Kafr el-Elow*

8. Kafr el-Elow Revisited: An Analysis of Continuity and Discontinuity of Change      127

*The National Scene: Egypt — The Local Scene: Kafr el-Elow — Conclusion*

Glossary      157

References      162

Recommended Reading      164

# Introduction

KAFR EL-ELOW is a peasant community located at the southern end of the Governorate of Cairo in the United Arab Republic, just eighteen miles south of Cairo, the capital of the nation. My first glimpse of the village came one day in October 1964, as I was traveling with a group of researchers from the Social Research Center at the American University in Cairo to tour the iron and steel factory in the area. The smoke rising from the chimneys of various factories around the village attracted my attention.

When a colleague and I visited Kafr el-Elow several days later to determine the feasibility of undertaking a research project in this village, I was immediately impressed by the stark contrast between the traditional and modern ways of life. On one side of the village the *fellaheen* (peasants) were tilling their plots of land with the same type of implements as those used by their ancestors hundreds of years earlier, while on the other side, a modern industrial complex was emerging. Similarly, some villagers were riding donkeys and leading water buffaloes to their fields while others were riding bicycles to their factory jobs or were waiting for the buses to take them to work. Moreover, there was an obvious difference between the western-style dress of the younger generation and the traditional garb (*jalabiya*) of the elderly villagers. It seemed clear that Kafr el-Elow would be a suitable example of the impact of industrialization and urbanization on traditional village life in Egypt.

To make a valid study of the community life of an alien culture is a difficult task. Not only must the researcher possess a thorough knowledge of the language, but he must also develop a relatively high degree of intimacy with, and sensitivity to, his informants. In order to achieve this intimacy and at the same time maintain objectivity, I combined qualitative research techniques—participant observation and the collection of individual case histories—with quantitative ones—structured interviews and government documents. I also possessed a great personal advantage for relating to, and empathizing with, my informants. Although I had never lived in Egypt prior to undertaking the research project on which this study is based, I was reared in Jordan, a neighboring Middle Eastern society, had visited the country on several occasions, and was thoroughly conversant with the Arabic language and culture. My training in scientific research methods was received in the United States, where I had resided for twelve years prior to returning to the Middle East in 1964.

A decade ago the population of Kafr el-Elow was average for an Egyptian village, but since that time it has almost doubled, reaching about 8000 people, due mainly to the influx of migrant workers seeking employment in the area adjacent

*General view of Kafr el-Elow*

to the village where Egypt's largest industrial complex has recently emerged. Since the advent of industrialization, many new patterns of behavior have diffused into the village, directly and indirectly, from urban areas. Consequently, when this comprehensive study of life in Kafr el-Elow is combined with data from both past and

*Northern entrance to the village*

*Typical street scene in the village*

*Traditional home (right section) in process of being
replaced by new structure (left section)*

future studies of other Egyptian villages, it should contribute significantly to a better understanding of the Egyptian way of life. I do not claim, however, that this study will depict all the varied aspects of Egyptian culture, even in the rural areas, for Kafr el-Elow is only one of more than 4000 villages in Egypt where over 80 percent of the society's population now resides.

The main focus of this study is on the manner in which industrialization and urbanization have affected social institutions in Kafr el-Elow; namely, how the village community managed to borrow and then integrate the new traits into a relatively peasant culture. In Chapter 2 I will examine the ways in which villagers earn their living. Chapter 3 will cover the kinship organization which has prevailed since the time when the village community was established in the mid-eighteenth century and which has produced a cohesive network of social relationships based on intermarriage. Islam is examined in Chapter 4. This all-pervasive religious force is discussed as an institution, and I have recorded my observations of its influence on the villagers' behavior. The importance of formal education in the community is dealt with in Chapter 5, particularly in terms of its effect of generating a new spirit of competition among the villagers. We shall see in Chapter 6 how the villagers of Kafr el-Elow have assumed a new political identity, that is, how the village is being integrated into a larger political unit such as the state.

┌─────┐
│  1  │
└─────┘

# The Community

## Geographical Setting

EGYPT is comprised of four regions: the Western and Southern Deserts, the Eastern Desert, the Sinai Peninsula, and the Nile Valley and Delta. The 550-mile, narrow valley of the Nile River, extending from Aswan in the south to Cairo in the north, includes some of the most densely settled (1500–2000 persons per square mile) agricultural land in the world (see Figure 1). It is also the region where almost all major cities, towns, villages, and the bulk of the country's industry are located. Although comprising roughly 4 percent of Egypt's total land area (400,000 square miles), the Nile Valley and Delta contain about 65 to 70 percent of the country's population. Near Cairo, where the Nile Valley ends and the Nile Delta branches north toward the Mediterranean, is located the village of Kafr el-Elow (see Figure 2).

Egypt is divided climatically into two zones: the Mediterranean, including the Nile Delta, and the Saharan, covering Upper Egypt (see Figure 3). The village of Kafr el-Elow is situated in the southern part of the former zone. There are, in effect, only two seasons: winter, the cool period from November to March, and summer, a period of intense heat from June to September, which is marked by the total absence of rain in the country. Winter temperatures in the village average 66 degrees Fahrenheit, and summer temperatures average 96 degrees. The humidity in Kafr el-Elow ranges from 51 percent in May to 70 percent in December. Rainfall is extremely slight in the area of the village, averaging only 1.2 inches per year.

March to mid-June are the worst months in the Mediterranean zone where Kafr el-Elow is located, because the annual Khamasin winds, originating over the western desert, blow over the area carrying hot, dry air and dust which almost obscure the sun on some occasions.

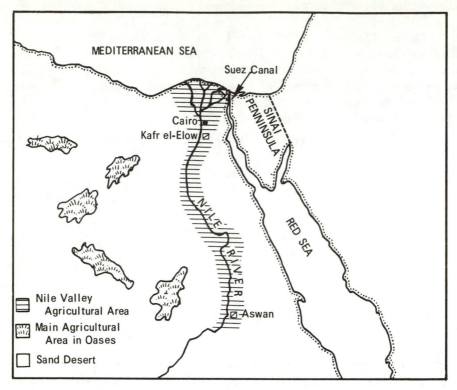

*Figure 1. Topography of Egypt*

## Physical Description of Kafr el-Elow

The village of Kafr el-Elow, located eighteen miles south of Cairo and five miles northwest of Helwan, is about three miles long and two miles wide. On the north, Kafr el-Elow is bordered by a citrus grove and by agricultural fields belonging to the neighboring village of Helwan el-Balad; on the south, just beyond some narrow fields, by the village of el-Tabeen located in the Governorate of Geiza; on the east, by a railroad track that leads to the Portland Cement Factory in the northwestern section of the village; and on the west, by the Nile River.

Four settlements constitute the village of Kafr el-Elow. While traveling south on the main road between Cairo and Kafr el-Elow, the first settlement one observes is ezbit enan el-baḥriya. Several hundred yards further south is the second settlement, ezbit enan el-qibliya, separated from the first by a road that leads from the main highway between Cairo and Kafr el-Elow. The third and largest of the four settlements, Kafr el-Elow, is located south of ezbit enan el-qibliya beyond a narrow strip of agricultural land and has two main sections. The northern section is inhabited by the descendants of Kafr el-Elow's first settlers, who belong to six different clans, each occupying a separate residential area within the section. The southern section (see Figure 4), inhabited until 1918 by Bedouin Arabs, is now occupied largely by migrant workers who started coming to this area during the decade 1955–1965.

Two small bridges lead from the main road across the canal bordering the nuclear settlement, Kafr el-Elow. The northern bridge leads to a road that passes through its northern section while the southern bridge leads to a road that passes through the center of the settlement, forming the dividing line between its northern and southern sections. Another road crosses the settlement from north to south. All these roads are narrow and unpaved. The canal separating this settlement from the

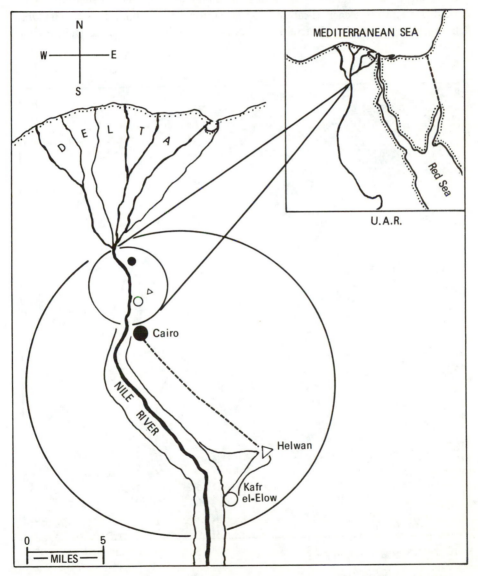

Figure 2. The location of Kafr el-Elow in the Governorate of Cairo, U.A.R.

main road is approximately five feet deep and fifteen feet wide. Water is pumped into the canal from the Nile River by a station located at the foot of the northern bridge, and small irrigation canals branch from this main canal into the agricultural fields behind the settlement. There are two public fountains here, one each on the eastern and western sides of its northern section, built by the government to supply the villagers with fresh water.

The Arabs who moved from the third or nuclear settlement in 1918 established the fourth settlement in Kafr el-Elow which is located at the extreme southeast side of the village adjacent to a sandy hill and is separated from the largest settlement by a fruit grove. This settlement, along with the settlements ezbit enan el-bahriya and ezbit enan el-qibliya, consist entirely of dwelling compounds. Only the nuclear settlement of Kafr el-Elow has both dwellings and public facilities.

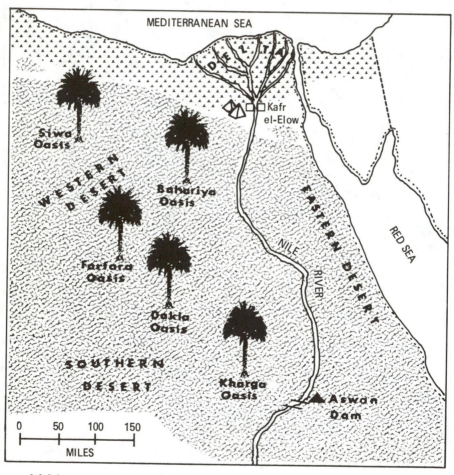

Mediterranean Zone

Saharan Zone

*Figure 3. Climatic zones*

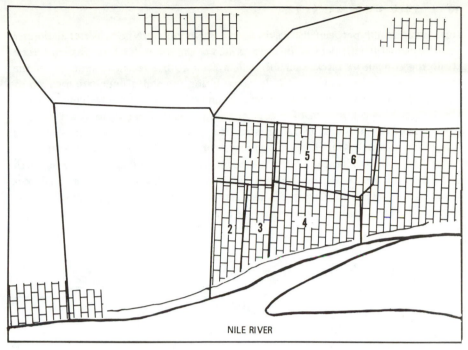

*Figure 4. The six residential clusters of Kafr el-Elow's six Hamula*

The houses in all four settlements are irregularly spaced, and many are situated close to the drainage and irrigation canals which cut through the village from north to south and from east to west. Additions have been made to many old residential structures and new homes are being constructed on land that was formerly used for cultivation. The former measure is viewed not only as a means of accommodating an expanding household and of maintaining family ties, but also as a status symbol, because such home alterations signify modernization.

The four settlements described above are treated as one community called Kafr el-Elow for the following reasons:

1. From an administrative point of view they are regarded as a unit, as indicated by their sharing one police station, one school, one mosque, and one cooperative society. The police station and school are located in the extreme northeastern section of the village, while the cooperative society is located at the center of the nuclear settlement.
2. There is daily, intensive interaction between the residents of the nuclear settlement, Kafr el-Elow, and those of the three surrounding settlements.
3. The village and its four constituent settlements comprise a single economic unit in that they share one cultivated area, one water canal system, and one market square. The latter, located in the center of the nuclear settlement of Kafr el-Elow, is the site of the entire community's shopping and economic transactions.
4. All major religious activities are carried out at the community mosque located in the center of the nuclear settlement. The four settlements also share the same burial ground.

Kafr el-Elow's agricultural fields are divided into two major sections separated by the main road running between Cairo and the village (see Figure 5). The fields lying east of the highway form a horseshoe around the nuclear settlement, while those on the western side of the highway, which are referred to as the Gezira, form a semicircle between the road and the surrounding Nile River. The former are sandy and infertile because they are located at the foothills of the Eastern Desert while the latter have black, rich soil which, prior to the recent completion of the Aswan Dam, was brought by the Nile River during the annual inundation season.

The new industrial development around Kafr el-Elow has significantly altered the ecological pattern of the village. Much land formerly devoted to agriculture has been allocated to factories and to new housing for persons who have migrated to the area for industrial employment. Only the cement and textile factories, however, are located within the boundaries of the village. At the northern end of the Gezira, where the Nile meets the main highway, there is a small port which is connected to Kafr el-Elow's cement factory by a single railway track. Cement is transported in small cars to the port for shipment by riverboat to Upper Egypt.

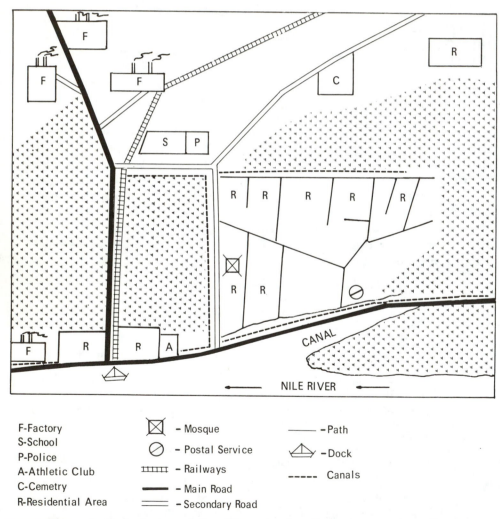

*Figure 5. General view of the village showing the various services offered*

Kafr el-Elow occupies a very strategic position, for it is situated only a few miles from Cairo where the Nile River branches out to form the Nile Delta. This delta forms a triangle, the base of which borders on the Mediterranean Sea. From a high point in Kafr el-Elow one has a clear view beyond the western bank of the Nile River to the Giza Pyramids, where one of mankind's oldest civilizations flourished over 5000 years ago. Moreover, Kafr el-Elow is linked to both the northern and southern parts of the country by the Nile River, and to Cairo, the capital and largest city in Egypt, by a paved road. This accessibility of transportation means has not only facilitated the marketing of cash crops by Kafr el-Elow's farmers, but has accelerated the process of urbanization in the village. It is Kafr el-Elow's geographical advantage, therefore, that accounts for those social and cultural conditions that distinguish this village from thousands of other Egyptian villages.

## Historical Setting

The village of Kafr el-Elow is located in a region popularly referred to as *masr*, the same term that has also been used traditionally to designate both the country of Egypt and Cairo, its capital. This implies that, to the Egyptian masses, Cairo is Egypt and Egypt is Cairo. Historically speaking, the region has been considered not only the political and cultural center of Egypt, but also of the entire Arab and Islamic world. Traditionally, and more specifically, Arabs view Cairo as a haven for both political refugees and scholars, and Moslems point with pride to the city as the seat of the famed Al-Azhar University, established during the tenth century, A.D., which became the academic center for Moslem theologians. The Egyptian people have made a continuous and highly significant contribution to world history from ancient to modern times, covering a period of well over 5000 years.

When compared to its region and the city of Cairo, the village of Kafr el-Elow is a "late arrival," for it was established only about 200 years ago. Yet the people of Kafr el-Elow identify strongly with the rich cultural heritage of their region, part of which is evident in the physical environment. The magnificent Giza Pyramids are constant reminders of the area's cultural background and historical significance.

The name Kafr el-Elow is derived from the Arabic word *kafr,* meaning "a clustering of people," and *elow,* meaning "height." Hence, the complete name may be translated as "the high village." According to the village elders, the original inhabitants of Kafr el-Elow were members of six families who initially founded a village called Nazlet Abou Darwish under the leadership of Ali Abou Darwish. The village was approximately one mile south of Kafr el-Elow; the inhabitants moved after it had become inundated by the Nile River. Upon resettling in Kafr el-Elow, Ali Abou Darwish not only continued to serve as the leader and spokesman of the six families, but also became the village head (*omda*), assuming responsibility for such official matters as taking the village census, solving disputes, and providing for the security of the community.

Many of the present-day inhabitants of Kafr el-Elow trace their ancestry to the villages from which the original six families migrated, and some still maintain contact with relatives in these villages, visiting them on holidays and other special occasions. The Dawudeya family, for example, came from Gamaleh village; the Boras and the Khalil families, from Sakkarra village; the Salloum family, from Moussa village; and the Ellahouni family, from Lahoun village. Until recently, Kafr el-Elow was popularly referred to as Nazlet Abou Darwish, in memory of the early village, although its official name has always been Kafr el-Elow.

Shortly after the population of Nazlet Abou Darwish moved to Kafr el-Elow in the mid-eighteenth century, the village head (*omda*) distributed the unclaimed land around the village among the eighteen households into which the founding families were divided and, as it was sandy and covered with bushes and bamboo (*tarfaya*) trees, ordered it cleared for cultivation. However, even the most fertile land in the village was not cleared for cultivation until the late 1930s, for traditionally, the Egyptian *fellaheen* have not been desirous of land ownership. In some cases, *fellaheen* who could not pay their land taxes refused to admit their rights to land claims due to the severe penalties imposed on those who failed to pay their taxes. Such unclaimed land, which became the property of the Royal Family, constituted half of the cultivated area within the village of Kafr el-Elow prior to the Revolution of 1952 and was planted mainly in citrus fruits. Following the Revolution, when the Ministry of Agrarian Reform took over the property of the Royal Family, several families in the village petitioned to reclaim the land which had been taken from their ancestors, but such claims were never recognized. Instead, the land was cleared of its citrus trees, divided into small plots, and rented to the *fellaheen* in the village.

While the agricultural situation in Kafr el-Elow has always presented a bleak picture, the value of industrialization was introduced there as early as 1918 when a small gypsum factory owned and operated by Salah Ennan was opened. Thereafter, a few villagers began to supplement their farm incomes by cutting gypsum from the nearby mountain for sale to the factory. In 1928, with the help of a Belgian company, Salah Ennan built the factory known today as the Helwan Portland Cement Company. Production started early in 1930, but it did not provide a significant source of supplementary income for the villagers, because total factory employment never exceeded 150 people and laborers were recruited not only from Kafr el-Elow, but also from neighboring villages. A small dyeing shop was opened several years prior to the establishment of the cement factory, but it employed only fifteen to twenty people for a relatively short period each year during the cotton season. After this business was in operation for about ten years, however, it went bankrupt and closed down. When it resumed operations in the late 1930s, it did so under the name of the Helwan Silk and Textile Company.

With the start of World War II in the early 1940s and the establishment of large British camps around Kafr el-Elow, an abundance of new employment opportunities was provided for people residing in the area. Many young men left agricultural work to take jobs in British camps as servants and laborers. During the mid-1940s, the Stilco Company was established to build river boats on a small scale, but most of the company's employees were skilled workers imported from nearby Cairo. Most of these sources of income came to an end, of course, with the termination of World War II.

Industrialization's impact upon the lives of Kafr el-Elow's villagers was not significant until the late 1950s and early 1960s when, as a result of the government's nationalization process, all private industries underwent tremendous expansion. The Helwan Silk and Textile Factory, for example, now operates on a three-shift basis and employs approximately 16,000 persons, and the Helwan Portland Cement Factory, which also operates on a three-shift basis, has over 1200 employees. In addition, many new industries have developed in the Helwan area since the Revolution of 1952, so that the entire industrial complex now employs over 100,000 people, about 1200 of whom are residents of Kafr el-Elow. As a result, agriculture, commerce, education, communications—indeed, all phases of life in Kafr el-Elow —have undergone considerable modification. This, in turn, has affected the life orientation—the values and attitudes—of the people to the extent that the *fellaheen* residing in the village today could be said to have one foot in the traditional social order and the other in the modern social order. The homogeneity which once characterized Kafr el-Elow is diminishing as innovations increase, but the transformation is a gradual one.

In 1966, Kafr el-Elow was incorporated into the city of Helwan, the administrative center for the southern part of the Cairo Governorate, and was thereby rezoned as an urban area. It is within and against this physical setting and historical background that the economic, social, and political life of Kafr el-Elow can be most advantageously perceived.

## Population

The village of Kafr el-Elow covers approximately four square kilometers of land stretching eastward along the bank of the Nile River and has a total population of 6608 persons. The population of Kafr el-Elow has been increasing steadily during the past three decades, from 2656 persons in 1937 to 4018 in 1947, and to 6608 persons in 1960. (*U. A. R. Census Book* 1937:20; 1947:15; and 1960:23).[1] Moreover, according to many village informants, the population of Kafr el-Elow increased by at least 40 percent between 1960 and 1966, due largely to the influx of laborers from various parts of Egypt who settled in the village because of its proximity to the nation's largest industrial complex and because of the low rents prevailing there.

The annual rate of population growth in Kafr el-Elow, however, is only slightly greater than that in the nation as a whole: 3.0 percent versus 2.8 percent. The relatively high annual rate of population growth in Kafr el-Elow and throughout Egypt can be attributed to high fertility rates, since the average life expectancy level is only 51.6 years for males and 53.8 years for females. Persons under twenty-five years of age constitute about 60 percent of the population—58.8 percent in Kafr el-Elow and 57.3 percent in Egypt as a whole—while persons over fifty con-

---

[1] The census is taken once every ten years in the U. A. R. The last census was supposed to have been taken in 1957, but was deferred until 1960 due to the Suez Canal crisis of 1956–57. The writer relied on secondary sources, such as the *U. A. R. Census Book*, because the relatively large size of the village made it impractical for him to conduct his own survey.

TABLE 1
POPULATION DENSITY TRENDS IN KAFR EL-ELOW, 1917–1960

| Year | Population | No. of Households | Density per Square Kilometer |
|------|-----------|-------------------|------------------------------|
| 1917 | 908 | 307 | 419 |
| 1937 | 2656 | 557 | 664 |
| 1947 | 4018 | 857 | 1148 |
| 1960 | 6608 | 1482 | 2006 |

Source: *U. A. R. Census Book* 1917:18; 1937:20; 1947:15; and 1960:23, respectively.

stitute only 9.8 percent of the population in Kafr el-Elow and 12.5 percent of the population in Egypt generally.

Population density in Kafr el-Elow, as demonstrated in Table 1, is about 2006 persons per square kilometer, compared to a density of 15,633.9 persons per square kilometer in the Governorate of Cairo (*U. A. R. Census Book* 1960:23).

As Table 2 indicates, the population of Kafr el-Elow and of Egypt generally is almost equally divided between males and females, although this tendency is obviously somewhat stronger in the latter case. This might be explained by the fact that Kafr el-Elow is primarily an agricultural and industrial community, attractive to males more than to females, while the sex ratio of Egypt in general reflects the influence of the country's large urban centers such as Cairo and Alexandria, where commercial, government, service, and professional occupations appealing to women are more prevalent, producing a more favorable balance between the male and female population.

Table 3 reveals the marital status of Kafr el-Elow's villagers of marriageable age in 1960. It is interesting to note that about the same percentage of males as females were married: 75.84 percent and 75.38 percent, respectively; the greatest discrepancies prevailed with respect to the "never married" and "widowed" categories. Whereas three times as many males as females—22.28 percent versus 7.20 percent—were bachelors, about sixteen times as many women as men—15.99 percent versus .91 percent—had been widowed. The difficulty many men encountered in gathering an adequate dowry accounts to some extent for the higher percentage of males than females who have "never married"; the fact that females are encouraged to marry at an earlier age than are males also tends to reduce the percentage

TABLE 2
SEX COMPOSITION OF THE POPULATION IN KAFR EL-ELOW
AND IN EGYPT AS A WHOLE IN 1960

| SEX | Kafr el-Elow | | Egypt | |
|-----|--------|---------|------------|---------|
| | NUMBER | PERCENT | NUMBER | PERCENT |
| Males | 3,528 | 53.39 | 13,068,012 | 50.29 |
| Females | 3,080 | 46.61 | 12,916,089 | 49.71 |
| Totals | 6,608 | 100.00 | 25,984,101 | 100.00 |

Source: *U. A. R. Census Book* 1960:23.

| Sex | Never Married | | Married | | Divorced | | Widowed | | |
|------|------|------|------|------|------|------|------|------|------|
| | NO. | PERCENT | NO. | PERCENT | NO. | PERCENT | NO. | PERCENT | TOTALS |
| Males | 390 | 22.28 | 1328 | 75.84 | 17 | .97 | 16 | .91 | 1751 |
| Females | 126 | 7.20 | 1320 | 75.38 | 25 | 1.43 | 280 | 15.99 | 1751 |
| Totals | 516 | 14.7 | 2648 | 75.6 | 42 | 1.2 | 296 | 8.5 | 3502 |

Source: *U. A. R. Census Book* 1960:210.

of females relative to males in the "never married" category. Widows, on the other hand, far exceed widowers, because it is not as socially acceptable for women to remarry after the death of a spouse as it is for men to do so. Women's greater life expectancy and difficulty in securing a mate after reaching an advanced age are other major explanations.

# Health

As I indicated in the previous section, the life expectancy level in Kafr el-Elow and throughout Egypt is low when compared to western standards. According to information provided by some elderly villagers and the medical staff at the village clinic, more than twenty-five percent of the children die before the age of one year, and those persons who survive to maturity generally appear much older than their ages would seem to warrant. Moreover, the physical conditions essential to good health are generally lacking. The unpaved streets are dusty during the summer and muddy during the winter, making it difficult to maintain clean homes. The absence of a sewage system encourages the villagers to dump their dirty water in the streets; children as well as animals defecate in the streets; and the village canal, where people wash their clothes and eating utensils, is used to dispose of all manner of waste material. Because the villagers have no screens on their homes, water and food are readily subject to contamination by flies, mosquitoes, and other insects which are particularly prevalent during the hot summer months. Moreover, lack of refrigeration causes food to deteriorate rapidly; therefore, food poisoning is an ever-present threat to the villagers. It is not surprising that tuberculosis, dysentery, typhoid fever, bilharsiasis, malaria, and other contagious and infectious diseases are common maladies. Eye infections are especially prevalent among the children; in 1966, thirty-four cases of blindness were reported in Kafr el-Elow.

Until recently, the *fellaheen* of Kafr el-Elow relied almost exclusively upon folk medicine to remedy various diseases. Besides the village barber who played the traditional health official role, administering first aid as the need arose, a few elderly women prescribed, upon request, folk "cures" (*wasfat baladiya*) for the sick. For example, they treated persons with severe headaches by cutting their skin at the point of greatest pain with a razor blade to relieve the blood pressure. In tonsilitis cases, they rubbed the patient's tonsils with coffee and lemon juice and, if this treatment failed, they attempted to sever the tonsils with their fingers. Persons with fever were rubbed with vinegar and salt and fed sour milk. Victims of burning were first rubbed with kerosene, then coffee powder was applied to the burned areas of their bodies. Toothaches were "cured" by putting fertilizer on the source of the pain.

Most of the villagers of Kafr el-Elow still tend to prefer these home remedies to the scientific treatment of illnesses and injuries. This is especially true of females who are frequently too shy to expose themselves to a doctor for a physical examination. Moreover, according to some informants, many men object to having their wives examined by the village doctor because he is a male. (There is no female physician in Kafr el-Elow.) Father Ayrout, who is founder and General Director of the free schools in the villages of Upper Egypt and has been called the Albert Schweitzer of the Nile, further explains this tendency:

> The ignorance and, still more, the poverty of the *fellah* make it difficult to take care of him. Medical stations and centers do exist, especially in Lower Egypt, and the price of the medications at these government centers is well within reach of most of the *fellaheen*. But the *fellah* goes to the doctor only when he is very ill, because it means the loss of a day's wages, the bus fare to the hospital, as well as the price of the medicine. If the medicine is not to be found in the store of pharmaceuticals at the clinic, he must buy it commercially for what is to him a great price. (Ayrout 1963:77)

Unlike the doctors at the government medical centers, those who practice folk medicine do not charge even a small fee for their services because they believe that by helping others they will be rewarded in heaven.

Despite the prevailing resistance to modern medical practice in Kafr el-Elow, an increasing number of villagers are resorting to trained physicians for treatment. This trend can be explained by several factors:

1. In the mid 1950s, when the village of Kafr el-Elow was under quarantine due to a smallpox epidemic, doctors remained there until the disease disappeared. This experience converted many of the villagers to an understanding of the value of modern medicine.
2. In 1959, a physician opened the first private clinic in Kafr el-Elow on a part-time basis, but the project failed due to lack of interest among the *fellaheen*. In 1963, however, another clinic was opened on a part-time basis, the doctor charging fifteen piasters for an office visit and twenty-five piasters for a home visit. While the majority of the clinic's patients are still infants and children, the doctor's presence in the village for a few hours twice each week has contributed to a gradual shift away from folk toward modern medicine.
3. The new industries which have recently emerged around the village provide medical treatment and drugs for their employees free of charge and to their employees' families at minimum cost.
4. More public clinics and hospitals, where the sick are treated free of charge, have been opened in the Helwan area adjacent to the village of Kafr el-Elow.
5. The mass media, especially transistor radios, have taught the villagers the importance of personal hygiene and of cleanliness in general.
6. The modern village elementary school, by checking its students' cleanliness each morning and by sending them home if they fail to meet certain standards, has made the villagers more conscious of and concerned about good personal hygiene habits.

There is no way to determine the percentage of Kafr el-Elow's villagers who now resort to modern medical treatment. More important is the fact that an inroad has been made by modern medicine which is certain to have significant consequences upon the health of the villagers. Kafr el-Elow is more fortunate in this respect than most other Egyptian villages in that its strategic location near Cairo and Egypt's largest industrial complex is enhancing the peasants' formal educational opportunities and is bringing contact with people from outside their village.

## Housing

As one drives from Cairo or Helwan and approaches the village of Kafr el-Elow, the first things that come into view are the clusters of dwellings separated from one another by narrow, winding, unpaved roads. There are three types of dwellings in Kafr el-Elow, the first or traditional type (*fellahi*) referred to by the villagers as *haush or daar*. The traditional type of dwelling usually has walls two or three feet thick constructed of unbaked bricks made with mud and straw, although a few prominent villagers' homes are constructed of stone. That the traditional style of home is well suited to environmental conditions in Kafr el-Elow is attested to by the fact that some of these homes are at least eighty years old. Breaks in the walls are repaired simply by an application of mud plaster covered with whitewash.

The only entrance to the traditional home is a large wooden door, closed at all times for the sake of privacy; on either side is often placed an earthen or wooded bench covered with straw mats or rugs where the males of the household sit and spend their leisure time. This door opens onto a wide, roofless, dirt-floored

*Traditional style house*

courtyard, the dimensions of which may vary from ten feet by ten feet to twenty feet by fifty feet, depending on the size of the house. The courtyard serves many functions for the household members. During the summer months, one corner is used as a kitchen where cooking is done on a kerosene or wood-burning stove. Dishes, eating utensils, and clothing are also sometimes washed in the courtyard, or are washed in the canal and then rinsed with clean water in the courtyard. The water is then carried in a pail to the entrance of the house where it is dumped in the street, due to the absence of a sewage system in the village. This is an unsanitary practice that frequently causes friction between neighbors living next door to, or across from, one another.

The household privy is still another facility located in the courtyard, usually in one of the corners. It consists of a small enclosure (approximately three feet by three feet) with a concrete floor constructed around a pit lined with stones and covered with a piece of wood. When the pit is nearly full of excreta, it is emptied by persons who make this task their principal occupation. The excreta is removed in buckets and is then buried in a hole in the street, in a vacant lot, or next to the canal, and is covered with earth. The collector digs a new hole each time he empties a privy, as there are no permanent waste disposal pits in the village. After the excreta has dried, it may be dug up and transferred to the fields to be used as fertilizer.

Other facilities that may be found in the courtyard of a traditional home are a cement wash basin (a recent innovation), a large earthen jar (*zeer*) for the storage of cold drinking water, a shelter (*zareeba*) for farm equipment and for livestock (water buffaloes, donkeys, goats, and sheep), and a chicken coop (*khoum*). Sometimes, too, jars or cans are hung on the walls of the courtyard as roosting places for pigeons.

Off the courtyard and adjacent to the main entrance of many traditional homes, is a room designed to accommodate male guests so that they will not come in contact with the female members of the household. The women leave the courtyard and retire to their rooms when male guests enter the house, but they often return to resume their work after the men have entered this room and closed the door behind them. The other rooms of the house are also located off the courtyard, but are further removed from the entrance.

Most homes in Kafr el-Elow are meagerly furnished one-story structures. Roofs on most traditional houses are constructed of rough wooden beams covered with sticks, bamboo, and straw; these, in turn, are overlaid with mud. The roof is frequently used as a drying area for both clothes and agricultural products. Inside are usually concrete floors and most homes have white-washed interior as well as exterior walls. Some traditional homes still have dirt floors and a few have two stories, the floor plans of which are essentially the same. The second floor, constructed of mud or cement and supported by steel beams, usually consists of one or two rooms used for storage or to accommodate guests or a newlywed son and his wife. During the winter, people generally sleep on cotton-filled comforters laid over straw mats which serve as insulation against the dampness; during the summer, however, when the coolness of the floor is desired, comforters are used without the straw mats. Before the villagers retire for the evening, they always secure the latches on their courtyard doors.

Inasmuch as there are no public baths in the village, one of the rooms in every traditional home is used for bathing, wherein the individual usually sits on a wooden stool, scrubs himself with soap, and then rinses himself by dipping warm water from a basin and pouring it over his body. The water is usually heated in a pan on top of a kerosene stove. Any room in the house may be used for bathing since there are no specific bathroom fixtures or appliances involved.

While prior to 1950 all homes in Kafr el-Elow were of the traditional type, at the time this study was completed (1966) not more than 70 percent of all dwellings in the village were of this style. Fortunately, however, most of the traditional homes are now electrically lighted; their small windows do not admit much natural light even though they have no glass panes.

The average size of the household in Kafr el-Elow was 4.5 persons in the mid 1960s, only slightly over the national average of 4.4 persons. In terms of density per room, however, Kafr el-Elow exceeded both the Governorate of Cairo and Egypt as a whole. Kafr el-Elow averaged 2.6 persons per room versus 2.3 persons per room in the Governorate of Cairo and 1.9 persons per room in Egypt in general. These comparative statistics reflect the relatively crowded housing conditions in Kafr el-Elow resulting from the influx since 1950 of workers seeking industrial employment.

This situation has encouraged those with sufficient capital to build new dwellings for their own use or for rental purposes, a tendency which has stimulated a tremendous amount of competition among relatives and neighbors. As one elderly informant told me, "This village is referred to as *balad ish-mina*," which means "If my neighbor, cousin, or other relative can build, why can't I do the same?" Building a new dwelling has become such an important status symbol in Kafr el-Elow that persons with limited financial resources sometimes construct their units gradually until they accumulate enough money to complete the project.

These new dwellings, which have made their appearance in ever-increasing numbers since the early 1960s and which constitute the second and third types of housing in Kafr el-Elow, are modern apartments and one-family homes constructed either of oven-baked bricks or of reinforced concrete and steel imported from outside the village. In structure and design they resemble urban dwellings in Helwan with their flat wooden roofs, glass windows, cement or tile-covered floors, electricity, indoor bathrooms and kitchen, and bedrooms outfitted with modern furniture.

In the past, when all the villagers lived in traditional homes with only one entrance, renting living facilities was considered an unacceptable practice, because it could have led to the exposure of the females in the family to strangers. Today, even some villagers living in traditional homes will rent rooms to married couples, but never to single men. Since each residential unit in the modern houses and apartments has its own entrance, there is no reluctance to rent these facilities to strangers. The monthly rent range in Kafr el-Elow is roughly one-half Egyptian pound to one Egyptian pound for a room and three Egyptian pounds to six Egyptian pounds for an apartment or house, depending on the size and condition of the accommodations. (One Egyptian pound—approximately $2.2.) For example, I rented an apartment consisting of three rooms, a kitchen, shower, and privy for six Egyptian pounds per month. Most of the modern dwellings are located in the southern part of Kafr el-Elow and cater primarily to industrial workers; this explains why new-

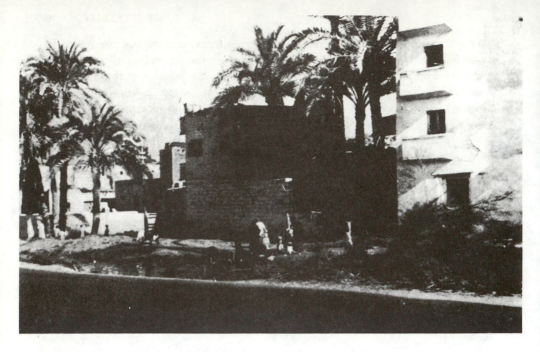

*Modern style housing*

comers, all of whom are employed in factories around Kafr el-Elow, are concentrated in this section of the village.

It is obvious, then, that expansion is the new trend in Kafr el-Elow with respect to housing and expansion is directed toward modern architectural standards. New modern dwelling units, which in 1966 constituted approximately thirty percent of all housing in the village, were being constructed to accommodate both newcomers and long-established residents, and many traditional homes were being renovated to add a touch of modernization or to accommodate expanding families.

## Clothing

The traditional dress for males in the village of Kafr el-Elow is the *jalabiya,* which resembles a man's nightgown in the United States, except that it is ankle length. The winter-season *jalabiya* is made from flannel or heavy cotton, while the summer garment is made from light-weight cotton or silk. It has a hip-level pocket on each side and an opening for the head extending downward about twelve inches from the neckline, which may or may not have a collar similar to that on a shirt. Worn over a cotton undershirt and knee-length shorts, the *jalabiya* is a very full garment which is easy to put on and take off. When working in the fields, the *fellaheen* usually take off the *jalabiya* and wear only their undershirt and shorts, because the garment might get wet or hinder their movement. During the winter they wear a vest over their undershirt for extra warmth.

Villagers who work in the factories are required by law to wear western-style clothing—a shirt and khaki trousers—or, as it is called in Arabic, *el-badla eshabiya* (national dress), because the *jalabiya* would be too apt to get caught in the machinery and cause an accident. Teachers and government workers also wear western-style suits. The majority of these workers, however, whether industrial, professional, or service employees, wear the *jalabiya* after returning home at night. One might say that the average male villager is an urbanite by day and a ruralite during the evening hours. The two village tailors who make most of the male villagers' clothing told the writer that the average man today has two *jalabiya*, and many have a third for special occasions, whereas two decades ago many men could not afford to buy more than one, although they sometimes shared a second *jalabiya* with male relatives within their households.

In contrast, younger generation males in the village, especially students, do not wear the *jalabiya*, preferring western-style clothing which they purchase in Helwan or Cairo. It is not surprising, therefore, that the three clothes-pressers in Kafr el-Elow, all of whom have opened their shops since the early 1960s, depend largely on the younger generation for business. Prior to 1960, anyone who wished to have clothing pressed had to take it to Helwan. Even today, shirts and trousers must be washed at home before being taken to a presser's shop. After returning home from work or school, many younger males wear pajamas to walk about the village; this is considered a sign of sophistication, inasmuch as the practice of wearing pajamas was adopted from urbanites. While a small cotton or woolen cap is worn by all elderly men in the village, most younger males prefer to go bareheaded. Shoes and sandals, however, are worn by most men in Kafr el-Elow, irrespective of age; very few walk about barefooted as in the past.

The only public dress considered appropriate for women who are long-established residents of the village is a black cotton or silk *jalabiya*, a symbol of maturity and stability, which is similar to the garment worn by men except that it is fuller. While young girls under the age of twelve are permitted to wear colored dresses anywhere, older girls and women may do so only in the privacy of their homes. On various occasions, however, I observed village women who had worn a *jalabiya* over a western-style dress while traveling on the bus between Kafr el-Elow and Helwan or Cairo take off the *jalabiya* upon reaching the city and place it in their handbags.

Women in Kafr el-Elow purchase the material for their garments either in Helwan or from a female peddler who comes periodically to the village, selling from door to door. Then the material is taken to one of the few dressmakers in the village who may charge from fifteen to twenty-five piasters for each *jalabiya* or dress. In public, village women also wear shawls over their heads, the ends of which they wrap around their necks. While shoes and sneakers are becoming increasingly popular among the women of Kafr el-Elow, some still walk about the village barefooted. Very few females in the village wear either western cosmetics such as powder, rouge, and lipstick, or local cosmetics such as *kohl* (eye makeup) and *henna*. Those who do are mainly young married women whose husbands are employed in urban occupations, and they purchase their cosmetics from a female peddler who comes to the village regularly from Cairo.

The fact that both students and newcomers—especially those from urban areas—wear western-style clothing has encouraged the older, long-established male villagers of Kafr el-Elow to make the transition from traditional to modern clothing. The few women who dare to wear western-style dresses in public, however, are newcomers and visitors, and they are frequently objects of ridicule, especially by the children in the village. While boys are required to wear western-style slacks and shirts and girls wear uniforms at school, they wear the *jalabiya* at home and at play.

# Diet

Traditionally, the majority of peasant families in Kafr el-Elow lived almost exclusively on bread (*aish*) made from corn and/or wheat that they raised on their small plots of land. Indeed, bread still constitutes the major item in the diets of some of the villagers, and for most people is an important accompaniment of every meal.

*Aish* is usually prepared in two different forms: the round, thin, dry variety (*battawi*) made of corn and fenugreek seeds, which is frequently referred to as *aish fellahi,* and the round, double-layered, soft type (*aish baladi* or *aish tari*) made of wheat, which is similar to the bread sold in urban areas. Although some of the *fella-heen* make their own flour from the wheat and corn that they raise on their small plots, the majority spend a substantial portion of their incomes to purchase flour from one of the four flour shops in the village. When a village family has its flour for making bread a year in advance, it feels very secure. Some villagers buy their bread from the commercial bakery which was established in Kafr el-Elow during the early 1950s to accommodate the migrants who came to work in the local industries. However, most of the bakery's customers, are single men, because it is usually more expensive for families to buy their bread than to make it at home.

## BAKING DAY (*Youm El-Khabeez*) IN KAFR EL-ELOW

Baking bread, a biweekly event in the village, provides an opportunity for women who live in the same *haush* (courtyard) to socialize and gossip. On that day, women from several neighboring families bake bread together at the home of one who serves as hostess for the occasion. The women begin to prepare the dough at their respective homes early in the morning, using their hands to mix together flour, yeast, and water. The mixing process is repeated over and over again until the dough ferments and is ready for baking: usually after about three to four hours. Then it is put in a large dish (*tesht*) and taken, around sunrise, to the home of the woman whose oven is to be used. After all the women have assembled, one starts burning fuel to heat the oven, while the others take pieces of dough and place them on the *matraha,* a flat, wooden plate with a long handle used to put the dough into the oven. Frequently, the women do the hostess' baking in return for using her oven and fuel. A professional baker may also be hired for about thirty-five piasters a day to do the baking, several families sharing the cost of her services as well as that of the fuel, which is usually *galla* (dung) and *kash* (straw).

## OTHER PROMINENT ITEMS IN THE VILLAGERS' DIET

Besides bread, the average villager in Kafr el-Elow today consumes meat (lamb and beef but no pork, because Islam forbids the eating of pigs' meat) or poultry once a week; local citrus fruits, watermelons, and cantaloupes; and vegetables, such as tomatoes, eggplant, cabbage, spinach, okra, squash, cucumbers, *mouloukiah*, and a variety of fava beans called *fuul*, which are high in protein content. After they have been soaked in water overnight, *fuul* beans are frequently ground, mixed with spices and parsley, shaped into small flat cakes, and fried in oil to make *tamiya*; this is often put between layers of bread, making a sandwich that is especially popular among Egyptian urbanites. *Fuul moudamas* is another bean dish currently popular among the villagers, tasting similar to chili and made by boiling *fuul* beans for a long time and then adding spices.

In spite of recent improvements, however, the villagers' diet is still mainly a starchy one, with little protein, fat, or sugar. Poultry is raised in the village, but primarily for commercial purposes rather than for home consumption; fish is seldom, if ever, eaten; meat is relatively expensive; and locally grown fruits are available only a couple of months each year. Daily meals are simple in content and are easily prepared. Women do all the cooking; men are seldom even seen in the cooking area of the house.

In most village homes, tea is prepared several times a day and is served between meals and with meals to members of the family and to house guests. Many shopowners in the village also serve tea to their customers. The tea is boiled until it is very dark and syrupy, then sugar is added, producing a very heavy, sweet drink. Yet, many villagers consume several cups in succession if the supply is adequate. Beer and soft drinks have only recently been introduced to the village of Kafr el-Elow and are consumed primarily by the younger generation, especially by those employed by industry. Beer is drunk in secrecy because the elderly villagers still adhere to the Islamic belief that the consumption of alcohol is sinful.

## RECENT TRENDS IN FOOD CONSUMPTION PATTERNS

Prior to 1950, the majority of peasant families in Kafr el-Elow had an extremely meager and unbalanced diet, consisting almost exclusively of bread. Meat was purchased only once every three or four months to celebrate holidays or special events, and then only in small quantities. Vegetables, too, were rarely eaten, because most of the peasants' small plots were planted in so-called "annual crops": wheat, corn, and barley. Most of the villagers purchased only kerosene, flour, tea, sugar, and soap from grocers. One of the village grocers told me that in the past, it was rare for a villager to purchase commodities with a five or ten pound note, and that it would have been difficult, if not impossible, for most grocers to cash such large bank notes. Today, however, the village grocers are accustomed to having their customers make larger purchases and are, therefore, prepared with a greater supply of currency. Moreover, the village grocers now stock a much greater variety of foodstuffs, including canned goods, soft drinks, and in some cases, beer, along with detergents, cigarettes, and many other household and personal items of the kind sold by stores in Helwan. Twenty years ago, such items could not have been sold in Kafr el-Elow. Today, the villagers in Kafr el-Elow purchase commodities from a variety of sources: from stores in Helwan and from peddlers as well as from the local grocers.

Three major factors have accounted for significant changes in the villagers' food consumption behavior since the 1950s: the shift of emphasis in agricultural productivity from annual crops to cash crops, such as vegetables, watermelon, canta-loupes, and citrus fruits; greater purchasing power due to increasing industrial employment; and contacts with migrants who have come from all over Egypt to work in the factories around Kafr el-Elow. The villagers have not only learned to include new food items in their families' diets through contacts with their migrant neighbors, but they have also acquired new techniques of preparing traditional as well as modern foods. It is too early to evaluate the long-term effects on health, mortality rates, and life-expectancy levels in Kafr el-Elow but, quite obviously, they should be positive.

## Public Utilities and Services

### WATER, SEWAGE AND ELECTRICAL FACILITIES

Prior to 1930, the villagers in Kafr el-Elow secured their drinking water directly from the Nile, women and girls carrying it in jars to their households. In the mid 1930s, however, the Egyptian government brought fresh water to the village by installing a public water tap at the entrance to the western side of the village. A second public water tap was installed during the late 1940s on the eastern side of the village. These two public fountains were the only sources of fresh water in the village until the early 1960s, when the government installed water pipes throughout the village to make it easier for villagers to bring water to their homes. At the time I was conducting this study, approximately 85 percent of the homes had indoor water taps. Nevertheless, women carrying jars on their heads going to and from the public fountains are still a common sight in the village, because the public fountains serve not only as sources of water, but also as focal points for women to congregate and exchange the latest gossip in the village. The public fountains are also used for washing clothing and utensils by women who do not have an indoor tap. Some are ashamed to admit this, contending that they prefer to use the public fountains so as to avoid making a mess at home.

The fact that mostly single women use the public fountains, however, leads me to conclude that another prominent function is served by going to and from the fountains; namely, this provides an excuse for unmarried women to walk through the streets of the village—which is considered inappropriate under other circumstances—where some eligible men might see them, inquire about their identity, and eventually marry them. Of course, going to and from the public fountains enables all women, irrespective of their marital status, to leave their homes and to observe for themselves the daily activities in the village. There is the additional consideration that water from the public fountains is free, whereas a fee is charged by the government for all water consumed through the indoor taps.

The public canals (*tura*), like the public fountains just discussed, are places where the village women congregate to gossip while they wash their clothing and kitchen utensils. Some women even use the canals for dumping human waste and garbage, because there is no sewage system in the village. Absence of a sewage system also results in the low-lying land's being inundated for months during the winter season when the Nile River level is high. Both situations constitute a health hazard because they contribute to the breeding of disease-carrying mosquitoes and flies.

Electricity was introduced to the village during the early 1960s. At the time of this study, most of the narrow streets in the village were electrically illuminated, and all the modern as well as most of the traditional homes were equipped with electricity. Electric power is used almost exclusively for lighting and operating radios; few homes have television, and I am not aware of the villagers' using any other electrical appliances. Most villagers use small bulbs for home lighting to reduce their electric bills.

## MAIL SERVICE

Prior to the year 1960, the small volume of mail coming into Kafr el-Elow was delivered weekly to the home of the *omda* for distribution. Most of the recipients were persons who came to the *omda's* home inquiring about mail which they anticipated from members of their households who had left the village for a short time. Outgoing mail was brought to the same place, the villagers giving the *omda* money sufficient to cover postage. Although the volume of mail in Kafr el-Elow has greatly increased in recent years due to the influx of industrial workers from distant areas, there is still no post office in the village. Instead, every morning a mail truck stops at a shop designated by the government to be the site at which mail is delivered and collected, with the exception of registered letters and packages which must be sent from, or picked up at, the post office in Helwan.

## TELEPHONE SERVICE

Before the mid 1950s, there was no telephone service in Kafr el-Elow; in emergencies the villagers had to use the telephone at the cement factory near the village. Since that time, however, telephones have been installed at the village police station, at the cooperative society office, and in the home of a laboratory technician employed by the cement factory. Although the cooperative society phone is available for public use, very few villagers have the need to place calls.

## TRANSPORTATION FACILITIES

The first modern form of transportation connecting Kafr el-Elow with Helwan and other neighboring villages was a taxi introduced in 1928. While the car was a novelty to the villagers at that time, very few availed themselves of its services because the fare—two piasters—was relatively expensive, considering that many of the villagers worked an entire day for that amount of money. In the mid 1930s, a bus line was established that connected a chain of villages, including Kafr el-Elow, with Helwan. This bus line made four round trips daily between Kafr el-Elow and Helwan, charging a fare of one piaster each way. Although the trip was short—a distance of about twelve miles covered in fifty to sixty minutes—it was an uncomfortable one due to the dusty, unpaved roads. Consequently, most of the villagers preferred to walk from Kafr el-Elow to Helwan, even though it took one and one-half to two hours to make the journey. A few villagers rode donkeys between Kafr el-Elow and Helwan.

Following the government's nationalization of the country's transportation system in 1957, not only did bus service between Kafr el-Elow and the neighboring villages become more regular, but also the principal road, connecting Cairo with Helwan and Kafr el-Elow's iron and steel plant, was paved. Prior to that year there were no paved roads in this area. Today a bus line operating on the main road between Kafr el-Elow and Helwan provides regular service every twenty minutes and extra express service during the morning and evening rush hours. The round trip takes about forty minutes and costs four piasters.

Although most of the factories around Kafr el-Elow provide bus transportation for their employees, many villagers prefer to walk or ride bicycles to and from work. Similarly, most farmers continue to use carts and donkeys to transport their products to market. The village school teacher has the only automobile in Kafr el-Elow, an old-model car which he uses not only for his own personal transportation needs, but also as a taxi to transport villagers in emergency situations and, upon request, to convey them to special occasions such as weddings.

# 2

# The Village Economy

PRIOR TO THE MID-1950's, the majority of the villagers in Kafr el-Elow earned their livelihood exclusively from agricultural work, cultivating their small plots of land for their own consumption or, as they expressed it, to secure the *munt il-bait* (basic food needed to maintain the family for an entire year). In recent years, however, rapid industrial expansion in the area around Kafr el-Elow, and the accompanying influx of migrants seeking employment in the factories, have produced profound changes in the economic structure of the village. Not only has a money economy developed in agriculture, whereby crops are raised for cash as well as for home consumption, but, as illustrated by Table 4, many new occupations have been created which now constitute the main sources of income for the majority of the villagers. With merely a cursory inspection of Table 4, one can easily see that only slightly more than 10 percent of the villagers were engaged in agricultural work in 1960, the remaining 90 percent being employed in other occupations. In this chapter I will describe the agricultural, industrial, and commercial sectors of Kafr el-Elow's economy and discuss the impact of each on the village social structure.

## Agriculture

### LAND OWNERSHIP AND INHERITANCE

In all agricultural societies where villagers make their livelihood mainly by farming, the people have a strong attachment to the land. This is true of, Egypt, too, where land ownership was and still is regarded as a source of security and as a status symbol within a community. Privately-owned land in the village of Kafr el-Elow, however, totaled only about 180 *feddan* (*feddan*=1.038 acres) until 1930, when another 120 *feddan* were reclaimed from the area bordering the Nile known as the Gezira. The 1937 population of 2656 persons in Kafr el-Elow relative to these 300 *feddan* meant that there was approximately one *feddan* for every nine inhabitants of the village. In 1960, the situation with respect to private land ownership in the village was much less favorable. While the population had increased to 6608

TABLE 4
ESTIMATES OF MAJOR OCCUPATIONS, 1960

| Occupation | Total |
|---|---|
| 1. Professional, Technical and Related Workers | 29 |
| 2. Administrative, Executive, and Managerial Workers | 5 |
| 3. Clerical Workers | 40 |
| 4. Sales Workers | 70 |
| 5. Farmers and Agricultural Workers | 380 |
| 6. Miners, Quarrymen, and Related Workers | 19 |
| 7. Transportation and Communications Workers | 31 |
| 8. Industrial Employees—Craftsmen and Production Workers | 1032 |
| 9. Service, Sports and Other Recreational Workers | 159 |
| 10. Workers Not Classified by Occupation | 2008 |
| Totals | 3773 |

Source: *U. A. R. Census Book* 1960:180.

persons, the total amount of privately-owned land had not changed since 1930, with the result that there was only one *feddan* for every twenty-two persons. Rapid population growth has resulted in continuous fragmentation of the land, making it difficult for agricultural productivity to keep pace with population needs.

The inheritance system in Kafr el-Elow is another factor which, through successive generations, has fragmented agricultural lands into even smaller units. According to the *Sharia* (Islamic Law), if a man dies leaving a wife, a son, and a daughter, one-eighth of his property goes to the wife and seven-eighths to his children; of the children's portion, a son's share is twice that of a daughter. In cases where only a daughter survives her father, she inherits half of the seven-eighths and the other half goes to her father's nearest male relatives, usually nephews. If the deceased is survived only by his wife, she is entitled to one-fourth of his property. When parents, as well as a wife and/or children, survive a man, each receives a sixth of his estate. If a man's parents are his only survivors, his mother is entitled to one-third of his property and his father to the remainder. The mother of the deceased will get only one-sixth of his property, however, if he has surviving brothers and sisters (Koran, Sura 4:11).

In practice, Islamic Law is not strictly followed with respect to inheritance rights. After a father's death, his sons usually divide the estate equally among themselves; only in rare instances do the daughters demand their share. While selling one's land to an outsider would be considered disgraceful, in cases where the individual land shares resulting from division are very small, one of the brothers may buy the others' holdings, sometimes simply to raise his status in the village. The importance of keeping landholdings within the family is also reflected by the villagers' preferring, when they are in need of money, to rent their land to tenants or sharecroppers rather than sell it. Another factor of significance in connection with land inheritance in Kafr el-Elow is the villagers' strong emotional attachment to their holdings, however small, for this is their only link with the deceased. Furthermore, parents take tremendous pride in the prospect of passing on property to their children, and for this they receive the villagers' respect.

TABLE 5
THE DISTRIBUTION OF ACREAGE AMONG KAFR EL-ELOW'S FARMERS, 1965

| Number of Farming Families | Number of Feddan Cultivated |
|---|---|
| 20 | 5-10 |
| 20 | 3-5 |
| 82 | 2.5- .5 |
| 170 | 1 kirat*—12 kirats |
| Total          292 | |

Source: Records of the village cooperative society and a survey I conducted in January, 1965.
* 1 feddan is equivalent to 24 kirats or 1.038 acres.

## LAND TENURE SYSTEMS

As I already indicated, the total amount of privately-owned land within the village of Kafr el-Elow is small—300 feddan—and land fragmentation resulting from rapid population growth and the inheritance system has prevented the emergence of any large farmers or landowners (see Tables 5 and 6). For this reason, the Agrarian Reform Law, enacted in 1952 to limit private ownership of agricultural land, did not alter the landholding situation in the village of Kafr el-Elow as it did in some other rural areas of Egypt. The law did, however, create a new system of land tenure based on the rental of land from the Ministry of Agrarian Reform, which now owns approximately 470 feddan in Kafr el-Elow, which were expropriated from the former Royal Family by the revolutionary government following its takeover in 1952. Three feddan is the largest plot, and one-half of a feddan the smallest, which a fellah may lease from the Ministry of Agrarian Reform. Rents under this new system are limited to seven times the tax on privately-owned land, and written leases, granted only to persons who will cultivate the land themselves, are binding for a minimum of three years. The 187 families in the village who lease land from the government either own no land or possess very small plots; priority is, I was told, given to the former (see Figure 6).

Traditional tenant farmers' rental practices continue, however, among those fellaheen who lease land in the village from private landowners. Rent varies a few pounds from the government's fixed rate of seven times the land tax, depending upon the fertility of the plot leased. The lessee may either assume complete respon-

TABLE 6
THE DISTRIBUTION OF ACREAGE AMONG KAFR EL-ELOW'S LANDOWNERS, 1965

| Number of Landowners | Number of Feddan |
|---|---|
| 12 | 5-10 |
| 20 | 3-5 |
| 70 | 1-3 |
| 167 | 1 kirat—1 feddan |
| Total          269 | |

Source: Records of the village cooperative society and a survey I conducted in January, 1965.

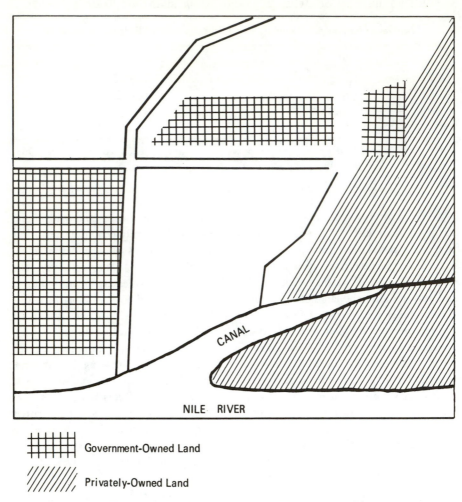

Government-Owned Land

Privately-Owned Land

*Figure 6. Land cultivated by villagers in 1966*

sibility for cultivating the land or enter into one of the following sharecropping agreements:

1. *The Musharaka (Partnership) Method:* The lessor pays for the seeds, fertilizer, the costs of irrigation and extra hired hands, if needed, and takes responsibility for marketing the crops. Any money remaining after the land rent has been deducted from the net income derived from the sale of the crops is divided between the lessor and the sharecroppers on a fifty-fifty basis. This is the prevailing sharecropping method in the village of Kafr el-Elow, although considerable risk is involved for both the lessor and the lessee when output declines or when crops are damaged.

2. *The Khumss (One-fifth) Method:* The lessor provides everything but the labor in the agricultural operation. When the crops are marketed, the lessor receives four-fifths of the gross income and the sharecropper receive one-fifth. Residents of Kafr el-Elow told the writer that they consider the *khumss* method degrading, because it is tantamount to performing a domestic service for the

lessor. Consequently, most of the sharecroppers who work under this arrangement come from outside the village.

A written contract is usually not involved when villagers enter into the private rental and sharecropping agreements described above, but the kinship system, as well as the network of social relationships among the villagers, imposes social and economic sanctions on those who violate such informal agreements.

## COOPERATIVE SOCIETIES IN KAFR EL-ELOW

The Egyptian Agrarian Reform Law of 1952 did not restrict its program to the redistribution of land, but, in addition, specified the establishment of agricultural cooperatives and compulsory membership therein for farmers who would rent government-owned land. The stated purpose of the cooperative societies is to render a variety of social and agricultural services in order to improve their members' standard of living. Among the important agricultural services rendered to the *fellaheen* by the cooperatives is the provision of certain essential farm supplies, such as fertilizer, insecticides, seeds, and animal feeds. These supplies are issued either for cash or on credit, with payment due when the farmer has marketed his crops. To secure the credit method of payment, the government cooperative in Kafr el-Elow has employed twelve guards and a supervisor who make certain that no *fellah* owing money to the cooperative markets his crops without first obtaining clearance from the cooperative's treasurer. If a *fallah*'s debts are longstanding, the cooperative may market his crops, deduct what he owes from the revenue, and give him the remainder.

The official staff of the government cooperative in Kafr el-Elow, which serves only 187 farmers—those *fellaheen* who rent land from the Ministry of Agrarian Reform—consists of an agricultural engineer, a treasurer, and a clerk, all of whom live in nearby Helwan and commute every day to and from the village. Besides these officials, the government cooperative has a ten-man council which is elected by the members of the cooperative for a three-year term and which submits the constituents' recommendations to the Ministry of Agrarian Reform through the cooperative office.

In addition to this government cooperative, there is a private cooperative in Kafr el-Elow which was organized in 1960 after a few farm owners petitioned the Ministry of Agrarian Reform for permission to establish a cooperative that would provide some of the benefits to them which the government cooperative was affording those farmers who rented land from the government. The five-man governing council of the private cooperative, elected by the 105 members (in 1966) for a three-year term, meets once a month under the supervision of an agricultural expert to discuss problems and suggestions submitted by the constituents. The agricultural expert has been assigned to the private cooperative by the Ministry of Agrarian Reform to render its official scientific advice. Moreover, every order that the private cooperative submits to the Ministry of Agriculture, whether for seeds, fertilizer, or other essential items, must be approved and signed by this agricultural expert.

When the private cooperative was organized, each member was charged one Egyptian pound in order to build up a fund with which to purchase spraying machines. These are rented to members as well as to non-members, although the former

*Villagers resting from harvesting*

are given priority. Later, shares in the private cooperative were sold to members for fifty piasters each, and the revenue was invested in seeds and fertilizer which are sold to farms on a cash or credit basis. At the end of each year, profits are divided among the shareholders in proportion to their investment in the cooperative.

### AGRICULTURAL LABOR

Agricultural work is almost exclusively a male occupation in the village of Kafr el-Elow. Most of the women who are seen working in the fields, weeding and picking vegetables, are hired laborers from surrounding villages or the wives of hired agricultural workers. The few female agricultural workers who are residents of Kafr el-Elow were described by the villagers as widows who are trying to earn extra money to take care of their own little plots. Under any other circumstances it would be considered disgraceful for a woman in Kafr el-Elow to labor in the fields.

When I was conducting this ethnographic study, many of the villagers cultivating from three to ten *feddan* complained to me about the limited availability of agricultural workers. This situation was difficult to comprehend at first, but with a more thorough knowledge of the village, it became apparent that Kafr el-Elow's location in the midst of Egypt's largest industrial complex affords more lucrative occupational opportunities in industry than in agricultural work. Another factor that makes farm work unattractive relative to factory employment is its seasonal character. Consequently, most of those in the village who are working as agricultural laborers are persons who are unable, for reasons of advanced age, sex (female), or physical disability, to obtain employment at any of the local factories.

The scarcity of persons available for agricultural work in Kafr el-Elow has produced the positive result of increasing farm wages. While a committee appointed by the Ministry of Agrarian Reform annually determines wage rates for farm workers in various sections of the country, the rates vary from twenty to thirty-five piasters for a nine- to ten-hour day, depending on supply and demand conditions in each area's labor market.

Egyptian law also encourages the formation of trade unions by agricultural laborers in order to promote their common interests, but there are no farmers' unions in the village of Kafr el-Elow. Most farm owners, however, provide their laborers with one meal daily (usually lunch), tea twice a day—during the morning and afternoon breaks—and a few cigarettes. These are what one might label voluntarily contributed fringe benefits, on the basis of which farm owners compete with one another to secure and retain their hired hands.

### CROP CULTIVATION AND PRODUCTIVITY

Today, as for centuries in the past, the *fellaheen* in the village depend entirely on the Nile waters to irrigate their crops throughout the year. The cultivated fields east of the main highway which passes alongside the village are irrigated by a canal which lies between these fields and the highway and by several smaller canals which branch out from it (see Figure 7). Water is brought to the canal from the Nile by a pumping station located in the village. The government maintains this irrigation system by including operational costs in the land taxes levied upon the

*Women who were working in the field*

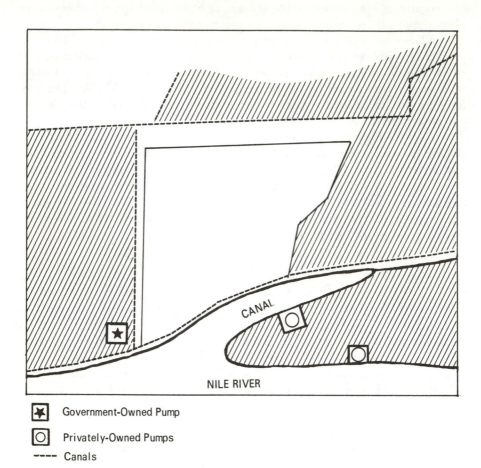

Government-Owned Pump ⬛★

Privately-Owned Pumps ⬜◯

---- Canals

*Figure 7. Areas served by irrigation canal systems fed by the Nile River*

*fellaheen* who own land in the eastern section of the village. Water for irrigation is automatically included in the rental contract of those villagers who rent land from the Ministry of Agrarian Reform. Once each year the canal is cleared of weeds, widened, and deepened by the Ministry of Irrigation so that water will readily pass through it.

The cultivated lands west of the main highway, known collectively as the Gezira, depend for irrigation upon two water pumps owned by three villagers, the irrigation process here operates on a systematic basis: *Fellaheen* who cultivate land in the Gezira area buy water for irrigation from the owners of the pumps nearest their plots. A certain number of cultivators are scheduled to irrigate their fields each day, the pump-owners timing every operation carefully and charging forty piasters each hour the machine is in use. Farmers located at a distance from a pump usually require more time to irrigate their fields than do those located close by, because part of the water is lost in the canal system before it reaches their plots. The *fellaheen* may either pay for their water at the time of use or defer payment until a later date when they sell their crops.

In regard to farm implements, most of the *fellaheen* have not progressed much beyond the primitive hand tools—rakes, shovels, hoes, and forks—employed by their ancestors. Only two farmers in Kafr el-Elow, each owning approximately ten *feddan*, have their own plows and draft animals. The other *fellaheen* hire one of the eight professional plowmen (*harath*) in the village to plow their fields. It still takes a plowman approximately four days to plow one *feddan*, but whereas in 1938 the fee was only one-half of an Egyptian pound per *feddan*, the fee in 1966 was between two and two and one-half pounds per *feddan*.

Other mechanical farm implements used by the *fellaheen* of Kafr el-Elow are the crop-spraying machines leased from the village cooperative societies and the pumps used for irrigation in the Gezira area. All this modern machinery must be purchased outside of the village because none of it is available in Kafr el-Elow as yet. While the *fellaheen* obviously continue to depend heavily upon ancient methods of farming, these modern techniques are better suited to the small plots cultivated by most of them.

Despite this heavy reliance on traditional farming methods, agricultural productivity is extremely high in the village: the *fellaheen* are able to harvest three to four crops each year. Throughout the year the *fellaheen* work in their fields almost daily, tilling, spraying fertilizer and insecticides, weeding, and picking crops to eat or sell. Vegetables such as tomatoes, beans, potatoes, cucumbers, squash, eggplants, and spinach, which are referred to as cash crops, are grown year-round in Kafr el-Elow, both for home consumption and commercial use. On the other hand, wheat

*Dredging silt from a canal*

and corn, referred to as annual crops, are cultivated on a small scale exclusively for home consumption, mainly for making bread. The farmers' plots are always green, but the intensity of the color is greatest—the vegetation is fullest—during the spring and summer seasons: March through August.

This agricultural situation is quite different from that which prevailed in the village prior to the 1950s, when the *fellaheen* raised not only wheat and corn exclusively for their own use, but vegetables such as tomatos, eggplants, squash, and cucumbers, as well. The revolutionary government, by first outlawing the cultivation of cotton which, prior to 1950 was raised on a small scale to pay land rents and taxes, and by then providing farmers with seeds and fertilizer, encouraged the present emphasis on the production of vegetables for commercial use. Other major causes are the increased demand for foodstuffs resulting from the expansion of the population since the late 1950s, and improved methods of transporting produce to market.

The *fellaheen* initially resisted the government-induced trend toward cash crops, fearing that the departure from the long-established tradition of annual crops might jeopardize their incomes, which depended, at the time, entirely upon farming. Gradually, however, they came to recognize the advantages of cash crops over annual crops, because raising the former does not involve crop rotation and long growing periods as does the latter, meaning greater productivity and more income annually. The prominence of cash crops in Kafr el-Elow's agricultural economy today is reflected in the recent construction by the Egyptian government of a refrigerated bin to store the farmers' seeds and potato cuttings for replanting at a later date. The farmers are charged a very small fee for this service.

## Methods of Marketing Crops

Since the late 1950s, when the *fellaheen* of Kafr el-Elow began to cultivate vegetables on a year-round basis, there has been a continuous flow of crops from the fields to merchants, a task which is usually carried out by one of four alternative methods. A group of farmers in the village may rent a riverboat or a truck to transport their crops to Cairo, where the produce is loaded on carts for delivery to various vegetable markets in the city. The crops may instead be transported to nearby Helwan by mule- or donkey-drawn carts, or, if the amount of produce is smaller, in boxes loaded on donkeys' backs. The trip from Kafr el-Elow to Helwan by this method takes slightly over one hour. The produce is occasionally sold to peddlers passing through the village who will pick up the crops from the fields, or the crops are sold to vegetable merchants in Kafr el-Elow. The latter two marketing procedures are used exclusively by small-scale farmers who produce crops mainly for their own consumption and sell the meager surplus.

## The Importance of Livestock

A considerable variety of livestock can be seen in the village: camels, donkeys, goats, sheep, cattle, and water buffaloes. Recently, due to the meat shortage in Egypt, cattle have become especially valuable commercially. Besides encouraging the *fellaheen* to raise more cattle, the government has also attempted to relieve the meat shortage by imposing a new restriction on butchers whereby they are permitted to sell meat only four days a week: Thursday through Sunday.

The government cooperative in Kafr el-Elow is attempting to relieve the meat shortage by periodically selling water buffalo calves to the *fellaheen* at a low price, at the same time sending a veterinarian to inoculate their livestock against disease free of charge. The private cooperative in the village is also making an effort to increase the meat supply by encouraging its members to raise more livestock and by providing them with feeds and veterinary services. In order to obtain these benefits, however, a *fellah* must register his livestock with the treasurer of the cooperative. At the time I was in the village, 800 head of water buffaloes and cattle, 25 camels, and 220 donkeys were registered with the village cooperative.

The government cooperative is also encouraging the *fellaheen* to raise more fowl for the commercial market by selling them month-old chicks at reduced price and by inoculating their poultry free of charge. As a result, chickens, ducks, turkeys, and pigeons can be seen almost anywhere one looks in the village: in the narrow streets and alleys and frequently inside homes. On occasions when I was invited to a villager's home in Kafr el-Elow, the host would frequently chase chickens and pigeons from the room.

Because the tending of poultry is strictly a female task in the village of Kafr el-Elow, income from the sale of poultry and poultry products usually goes to one of the women in the household: the grandmother, the mother, an aunt, or a daughter, depending on who purchased the baby chicks and nurtured them to maturity or market-readiness. A mother will often use poultry money to buy luxury items, such as gold jewelry, for herself or her unmarried daughters. For many widows and divorcées, however, poultry money is the only means of support. Rather than being sold for cash, poultry and poultry products are sometimes sold to a grocer on a barter basis; that is, they are traded for items such as sugar, tea, soap, needles, or thread, which the housewife needs personally or for family use.

The few sheep and goats in the village are raised for one of two purposes: to sell or to slaughter for home consumption during *eid-il adha*, an Islamic holiday when those who are financially able are expected to kill a goat or a sheep and distribute the meat to the poor. Camels are owned by only four villagers, and are used to carry heavy loads such as livestock, at which time the owner deducts the amount loaned plus a 5 to 10 percent commission, but no interest is charged.

# Industry

The *fellaheen* living in the village of Kafr el-Elow had their first industrial experience with the establishment of several small factories in the nearby Helwan area during the second and third decades of the twentieth century. However, prior to the Revolution of 1952, which inaugurated a period of accelerated technological development, the impact of industrialization on their lives was negligible. The following is a list of the principal industries which have either come into existence

TABLE 7
INCOME FROM THE AGRICULTURAL AND INDUSTRIAL SECTORS OF
THE EGYPTIAN ECONOMY, 1945–1952 AND 1952–1963
(EXPRESSED IN MILLIONS OF EGYPTIAN POUNDS)

| Year(s) | Agriculture | Industry and Electric Power |
|---|---|---|
| 1945 | 200 | 60 |
| 1952–53 | 252 | 127 |
| 1953–54 | 262 | 140 |
| 1954–55 | 301 | 155 |
| 1955–56 | 312 | 170 |
| 1956–57 | 374 | 192 |
| 1957–58 | 381 | 218 |
| 1958–59 | 364 | 240 |
| 1959–60 | 405 | 269 |
| 1960–61 | 403 | 297 |
| 1961–62 | 441 | 344 |
| 1962–63 | 469 | 376 |

Source: Khairi, 1965:302–303.

or undergone major expansion since the Revolution and are located within a radius of ten miles from the village of Kafr el-Elow:

The Egyptian Iron and Steel Plant
The Coke and Chemical Gas Company
The Misr-Helwan Textile Industry
The Helwan Cement Factory
The Misr-Spare Parts Manufacturing
  Company
The Stelke River-Boat Company

The Ceemaf Railway Wagons Ind.
The Steel Pipes Industry
The Aircraft Industry
The Military and Ammunition Complex
The Nasr Automotive and Tractor
  Industry

Table 7 reflects the gradual increase in Egypt's net income between 1946 and 1963 as a result of increasing emphasis on the industrial sector of the economy.

## POSITIVE RESULTS OF INDUSTRIALIZATION

Several major advantages have accrued to the *fellaheen* of Kafr el-Elow as a result of the industrialization process in the Helwan area.

JOB AVAILABILITY  Industrialization has given the residents of Kafr el-Elow greater job security, a condition which is rare in underdeveloped nations such as Egypt. In unindustrialized Jordan and Lebanon, for example, there is a shortage of positions for the available supply of technicians. Consequently, their surpluses of technically trained people are exported to the oil-producing countries of the Middle East: Kuwait, the Arabian Peninsula, and Libya. This is not the case in Egypt, however, especially around Kafr el-Elow, where those who acquire a technical education can easily find jobs in the new industrial establishments.

INCOME SECURITY  Because industrial employment is available within a short distance from Kafr el-Elow, it is possible for many villagers to continue cultivating their small plots of land after factory hours and on weekends, thereby supplementing their principal source of income and maintaining a financial cushion against unemployment.

*General view of textile mill from the village*

FRINGE BENEFITS  Industrialization has meant free medical care and drugs for all factory workers and their families in Kafr el-Elow. Retirement plans, whereby employers contribute to a general government fund for the workers' old age subsistence, constitute still another fringe benefit of the industrialization process in the village. In addition, the Egyptian government offers industrial workers a savings plan through the factories where they are employed; this is, at the same time, intended to curb inflation.

*General view of the cement factory from the village*

CONTINUANCE OF FAMILY SOLIDARITY    Since the industries in the Helwan area are very close to the village of Kafr el-Elow, it is not necessary for factory workers to leave their homes and families for weeks at a time, as would be the case if they were employed in some urban center such as Cairo. Nor is it necessary for them to undergo the problems of moving their families to such an urban setting. This, in itself, would be an expensive project, and would entail a continually higher cost of living besides. In addition, if forced to move, family members would likely experience cultural shock in making the transition from a rural to an urban environment. As Professor Watson has expressed it, "Migrant industrial laborers, parted from their relatives in the country, are in a way living in exile, for the atmosphere of the city is always alien to them" (Watson 1958:195).

The industrial situation around Kafr el-Elow also contributes to the maintenance of paternal authority in the family, because the husband and father returns home every day after work to exercise his role as head of the household: as the chief decision-maker, disciplinarian, and value-transmitter. Moreover, since single as well as married males can live at home while employed in the Helwan industries, young men are likely to marry girls from the home village, thus perpetuating the traditional endogamous marriage · pattern in Kafr el-Elow. Finally, kinship ties, whereby families within the same lineage depend upon one another regularly for companionship and for assistance in times of crisis, are more easily maintained when proximity of residence is made possible by the availability of ample employment opportunities in and around the village, as is the case in Kafr el-Elow. Professor Margaret Mead has stated the double-barreled advantage of such a situation in the following words:

> The waste in human welfare which came into being as a by-product of industrialization has caused much concern among governments, social scientists, and foundations. There appears to be general agreement that decentralization of industry—bringing work to the village or to its vicinity, within the framework of known associations and associational ties—will make for less disruption and, at the same time, will bring the increase in income needed for raising the standard of living. (Mead 1954:267)

NEW PERSPECTIVES    Villagers employed in the Helwan industries, by virtue of their daily contacts with workers from urban areas, are exposed to ways of life completely different from the traditional folk life prevalent in Kafr el-Elow. Moreover, they learn more about world events and about economic and political organization through their membership and participation in government-sponsored labor unions and in the Arab Socialist Union. All of these new experiences are then communicated by the workers to members of their immediate family, to relatives and friends, thereby multiplying the socializing effects of industrialization in the village.

STIMULATION OF THE LOCAL ECONOMY    Since its incorporation into Helwan's industrial complex, Kafr el-Elow's rural economy has received a larger cash income, because as well as investing, workers now spend an increasing amount of money on consumer goods to satisfy their newly-acquired tastes in food and clothing. Both tendencies have greatly reduced the incidence of economic deprivation in the village and have added a commercial sector to the economy wherein money, rather than barter, is the principal basis of trade.

GREATER SOCIAL MOBILITY   Evidence from informants and the case histories which I compiled in the village indicate that there is an increasing amount of intergenerational occupational mobility as well as career mobility, whereby a worker may change his occupation one or more times during his life, each new position bringing him higher income and social status.

The increasing opportunities for occupational and social mobility in Kafr el-Elow are reflected in the answers to the following questions which were posed to the villagers: "Do you think that the social position an individual attains is the result of his own efforts or the result of God's Will?" and "If you could start your life again, would you pursue the same employment path or change it?" In reply to the former question, 90 percent of the respondents said that one's social position is dependent upon his personal efforts; only 10 percent expressed the belief that it is predetermined by God (*kismah wa naseeb*). Therefore, it is not surprising, that 74 percent of the respondents to the second question said they would pursue higher education if they could begin their lives again, and 18 percent said they would seek more skilled employment; a mere 8 percent said they were satisfied with their position in life, and most of these, as one might expect, expressed the belief that no matter how hard a man struggles to compete, he cannot improve himself because his destiny is predetermined by God. In general, industrial employment is the occupational preference of the villagers, because it provides greater security, in the form of steady income and fringe benefits, than does operating one's own business or farming.

Three samples of life histories from the villagers of Kafr el-Elow clearly demonstrate that industrialization of the Helwan area has effected a significant amount of educational, occupational, and social mobility. The individuals selected for the first sample were those living in households where a grandfather, father, and son were available for interviews; those selected for the second sample were living in households where a father and son were available for interviews; and those selected for the third sample were villagers with whom I had frequent contacts. The first two samples provided evidence of intergenerational mobility, as demonstrated by Figures 8 and 9, while the third sample of case histories provided evidence of career mobility among individuals, as demonstrated by Figure 10.

As Figures 8 and 9 indicate, the two- and three-generation life histories collected in the village reveal an insignificant amount of intergenerational mobility —educational, occupational, and hence, social—from the first to the second generation, but a highly significant amount from the second to the third generation. It is especially interesting to note that none of the third generation was involved in agricultural work, reflecting the decline in the popularity of this occupation, as was discussed in the previous section. Industrial employment has become the prime occupational preference of the younger generation because of its association in their minds with affluence and the urban, modern way of life.

Similarly, Figure 10 indicates that no individual in the third life history sample remained in farming throughout his working life. Instead, 60 percent of the cases reflected career mobility: a change in occupation from the beginning to the end of the individual's work history. Finally, comparing the evidence in Figure 10 with that in Figures 8 and 9, one must conclude that career mobility among individuals is a much less conspicuous trend than is intergenerational mobility in the village of Kafr el-Elow.

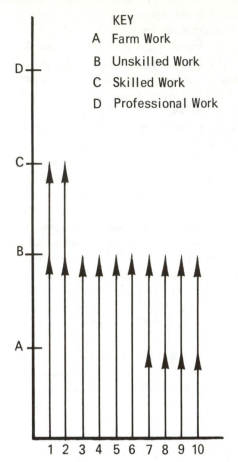

KEY
A  Farm Work
B  Unskilled Work
C  Skilled Work
D  Professional Work

*Figure 8. Comparative intergenerational mobility: grandfather–father–son*

NEW RECREATIONAL PATTERNS  Industrialization of the area in which Kafr el-Elow is located has also had its impact upon the use of leisure time in the village. New forms of recreational activity, reflecting the influence of technological progress, urbanization, and increased purchasing power, have become popular with many villagers, especially with the younger generation and with those who work in the local industries.

In the past, young men usually gathered on summer evenings in a field or, if the weather were inclement, at the village coffee shop (*gurza*) where they would play cards. While young people were aware of the recreation available in Cairo and Helwan, they usually confined their social activities to the village due to a lack of money and the strong opposition of their parents, and elderly relatives and acquaintances. On rare occasions such as holidays, however, some young people would go secretly to Cairo or Helwan to see a movie. Today, when more young people are financially independent and work away from home, it is a fairly common practice for them to attend movies in Cairo or Helwan; they still tend to conceal this fact from their parents, most of whom continue to regard this activity as sinful.

Another favorite pastime of today's village youth is congregating at their athletic club (*nadi il-shabab al-riadi*), which has a membership of about eighty persons ranging in age from twelve to twenty-seven, most of whom are students or factory workers. Leadership positions at this organization, however, tend to be dominated by the few members who are college graduates. The club is located on a piece of land that was originally given to the village youths by the Ministry of Culture and Guidance for use as a football field, but they obtained permission from the government in 1963 to build a recreation center on the site. Constructed with mud bricks by the young people themselves, the one-room center features two major types of recreational activity: soccer and table tennis. There are two soccer teams in the club—the junior and senior teams—which compete on weekends with teams from neighboring villages. Besides engaging in sports activities, members of the club also enjoy spending their time in conversation. Many students go to the center immediately after school each day, for fear that if they go home first, their parents will prevent them from going. Parents tend to view the center as a negative influence on their children, as a place where they will learn to smoke, will talk about "bad things," and will be encouraged to attend movies. For this reason, the young people of the village had to bear the entire financial burden for building their recreation center; their parents refused to contribute any money to the project.

Reflecting the impact of technological progress on the village, television and listening to the transistor radio have become popular forms of entertainment among people of all age groups. Since the number of television sets in the village is extremely limited, small groups tend to assemble from time to time at homes of those who have them. Listening to the radio, on the contrary, tends to be much

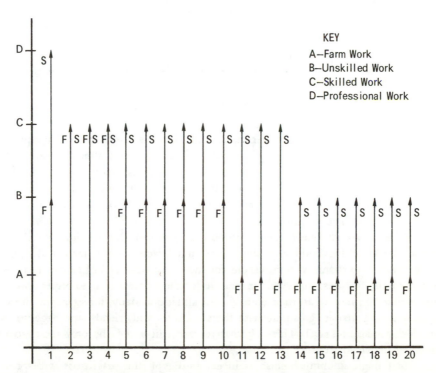

*Figure 9. Comparative intergenerational mobility: father–son*

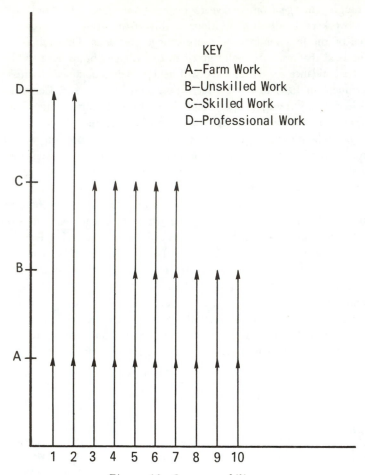

KEY
A—Farm Work
B—Unskilled Work
C—Skilled Work
D—Professional Work

*Figure 10. Career mobility*

more individualized because ownership of transistor radios is more widespread. While all age groups enjoy using the radio, elderly persons almost always tune into stations broadcasting religious songs and recitations from the Koran. If a young person dared to change the dial setting from a station broadcasting a religious program to one broadcasting secular music, he would be viewed as a sinner by his elders and held in disregard.

The area industries provide still other recreational activities for all age groups in Kafr el-Elow, although their recreational facilities—football fields, playgrounds, and club rooms with provisions for indoor games—are, of course, reserved for employees' families. However, the majority of the workers seem to prefer leisure-time activities unrelated to their employment situation. Many, for example, simply enjoy watching people, gossiping with their relatives and friends, and haggling at the weekly market (*suq*). These alternatives are still about the only recreational outlets available for females.

Although smoking hashish is illegal in Egypt, the practice is widespread throughout the country. In Kafr el-Elow, there are several private groups consisting

*Soccer team in the village*

of eight to ten men, mainly factory workers and government employees, who assemble once or twice a week to smoke hashish (or, more rarely, opium); this is done behind closed doors, because the practice is generally criticized by the villagers. Groups purchase hashish for these occasions from secret agents in the village, paying for it at the end of each month when they receive their salary checks. Although beer is sold openly in two village grocery stores, it, too, is consumed in secrecy and largely by young industrial workers. Elderly persons regard beer-drinking as "sinful" because Islam forbids the consumption of alcoholic beverages.

The two coffee houses in Kafr el-Elow are prominent social spots for industrial workers seeking legitimate or approved entertainment, since they serve only tea, coffee, and soft drinks. I was told, however, that a third coffee house in the village had been closed by the security police several years before my arrival because it was caught serving hashish to its customers. Card playing is the favorite pastime of coffee house patrons.

Industrialization has, as we can see, introduced the villagers of Kafr el-Elow to many new forms of entertainment—television viewing, radio listening, beer drinking, movie going, and athletic events sponsored by private clubs and factories —by increasing their leisure time, purchasing power, mobility, and contact with urban areas and peoples. Younger and better educated males, factory workers, and government employees—those villagers directly exposed to industry—have been the principal beneficiaries of thse innovations; elderly persons and women have been relatively unaffected by modern recreational patterns in the village.

## Negative Results of Industrialization

**Health Hazards**   The effects of industrialization on the village of Kafr el-Elow have not all been positive, however. Farmers frequently complain that their crops are damaged by smoke from the industrial establishments surrounding the village, particularly that from the cement factory. An agricultural engineer at the village cooperative society verified the farmers' grievances, stating that the cement dust is especially deleterious to crops on a windy or a misty day, because these conditions contribute to its reaching more crops and adhering to those it touches. Many villagers also complain about the human health hazard presented by the dust from the cement factory.

SOCIAL CONFLICT  The tremendous influx of migrants to work in the industries surrounding Kafr el-Elow has elicited a negative reaction from many natives who resent the newcomers for competing with them for jobs, for customers, and for marriage mates. A barber shop, tailor shop, butcher shop, and several grocery stores in the village are operated by new residents of Kafr el-Elow. Moreover, informants told me that several native youths had gotten into fights with newcomers over the latter's attempts to attract or flirt with native girls. As a result, some of these migrants had been beaten and forced to leave the village permanently.

## Commerce and Other Sources of Income

### THE GROWTH OF PRIVATE ENTERPRISE IN KAFR EL-ELOW

Transportation facilities are much better today than they were in the past; one can travel by bus from Kafr el-Elow to Helwan in approximately twenty minutes and by electric train from Helwan to Cairo in about an hour. Many villagers find it attractive to do their shopping for major items such as clothing in these large urban areas, where there is a greater variety and a better quality of merchandise. At the same time, commercial activity in the village of Kafr el-Elow has increased at an unprecedented rate in recent years.

Commercial activity in Kafr el-Elow prior to 1950, from the standpoints of both consumption and investment, took place at a very slow pace due to the impoverished economic condition of most of the villagers. As Table 8 indicates, seventy percent of the businesses established in Kafr el-Elow between 1920 and 1950 catered exclusively to the villagers' food needs. Since 1950, however, with rapid industrialization of the area around Kafr el-Elow and the accompanying increase in the villagers' purchasing power and level of expectation, not only a larger number but also a greater variety of businesses have been established in the village. Twenty-four new businesses were added in the decade 1950–1960 and thirty-five between 1960 and 1966 (see Table 8), bringing the total number of businesses in Kafr el-Elow to seventy-seven.

While it is true that the villagers' consumer activity has increased as their economic condition has improved, the major factor accounting for the tremendous growth of private enterprise since 1950 has been the villagers' greater capacity for saving, as well as their changing attitude toward investment. In the past, subsistence was all that could be expected from the villagers' meager earnings: savings were extremely small, or, as in the case of many families, non-existent. Land and gold jewelry were the most common forms of investment by those with savings; many, however, simply hid their savings under the floor, in a pillow or mattress, or in some other presumably "safe" place in the house. Today, a considerable number of families in Kafr el-Elow have savings, especially those with two or more mem-

TABLE 8
BUSINESS UNITS ESTABLISHED IN KAFR EL-ELOW, 1920–1966

| Type of Business | 1920–1930 | 1930–1940 | 1940–1950 | 1950–1960 | 1960–1966 | Totals |
|---|---|---|---|---|---|---|
| Groceries | 2 | 1 | 5 | 9 | 9 | 26 |
| Hardware Stores | – | – | – | 2 | 4 | 6 |
| Radio Shops | – | – | – | – | 2 | 2 |
| Electric Supplies Dealers | – | – | – | 1 | 1 | 2 |
| Tailors | 1 | 1 | – | 1 | 1 | 4 |
| Barbers | 1 | – | 1 | – | 3 | 5 |
| Coffee Shops | – | – | 1 | 1 | – | 2 |
| Pressers | – | – | – | – | 2 | 2 |
| Vegetable Stands | – | – | – | – | 3 | 3 |
| Shoe Repair Shops | – | – | – | – | 2 | 2 |
| Other Repair Shops | – | – | – | 1 | 2 | 3 |
| Bicycle Shop | – | – | – | – | 1 | 1 |
| Butcher Shops | – | – | 2 | 5 | 2 | 9 |
| Kerosene Dealers | 1 | – | – | – | 1 | 2 |
| Bakery | – | – | – | 1 | – | 1 |
| Flour Dealers | 1 | – | 1 | 2 | 1 | 5 |
| Sandwich Shops | – | – | – | 1 | 1 | 2 |
| Totals | 6 | 2 | 10 | 24 | 35 | 77 |

Source: Survey I conducted of all shop-owners in the village in November 1966.

bers employed by industry. When I inquired of several such families about their savings objectives, most replied that they planned to invest the money by either opening a small business, building a home for rental purposes, or establishing a savings account through the factories where they worked. A bank savings account was not frequently mentioned as an objective because there are no banks in Kafr el-Elow, where lending money with interest is still considered sinful. If a villager decided to open a bank account, it would be necessary for him to patronize the one bank in Helwan or one of many financial institutions in Cairo.

In recent years, the Egyptian government has been urging its citizens to invest as large a portion of their incomes as possible in an effort to stimulate industrialization and curb inflation. The growing spirit of competition among the younger generation, a probable by-product of the industrialization process, is another important factor explaining the relatively new enthusiasm about investment in Kafr el-Elow, a tendency which has been augmented by the influx of migrant workers from various part of the country. This spirit of competition was expressed to me by several village informants in the following terms: "If a thing is done by one person, there is no reason why it should not be done by others," *balad ish mina.* Many villagers, for example, compete with one another to provide housing facilities for the newly-arrived industrial workers, who find it cheaper to live in Kafr el-Elow than in Cairo or even Helwan. When a villager is planning a business venture of some sort, he may not publicize it for fear of the "evil eye," in other words, for fear that his neighbors' jealousy may cause his investment enterprise to fail. (The evil eye will be discussed further in Chapter 4.)

## Types of Occupations and Commercial
## Activities in Kafr el-Elow

There are several precise divisions which can be made separating one type of commercial activity from another; though these schemes are internally clear-cut, they tend to overlap with one another. Occupations and commercial activities in Kafr el-Elow may be categorized as traditional or modern on the bases of how long they have existed in the village and whether they operate using both barter and cash or exclusively cash. Another classification scheme is based on the place from which the service is rendered or the business transacted. There is also, interestingly enough, a clearcut dichotomy between dignified and undignified occupations in Kafr el-Elow. Dignified work consists mainly in cultivating one's own plot of land, performing one's own daily domestic chores, or helping a friend or neighbor with his field work and domestic tasks without receiving monetary compensation. On the other hand, jobs such as shoe repairing, barbering, and emptying waste pits are regarded as undignified and are, therefore, reserved for newcomers: principally for migrants from other rural areas of Egypt. That this distinction between dignified and undignified types of labor also exists in other Egyptian villages is illustrated by the reply which the shoe repairman in Kafr el-Elow made to me when asked if he would engage in the same occupation in his home village: "I'd rather die."

Most significant in the context of this book is the differentiation between traditional and modern commercial activity.

### TRADITIONAL OCCUPATIONS

THE VILLAGE BARBERS (MOUZAYIN)   The two "traditional barbers," who are brothers living in Kafr el-Elow, regularly cut customers' hair both at their shop

*Village shoe repairman*

and in their own home. Upon request, they will even go to their customers' houses or to the fields to cut hair. Because very few of their primarily elderly customers pay cash, the barbers must go to their customers' fields at the end of each crop season and receive compensation for their services mainly in wheat and corn. They are frequently given other farm products such as vegetables and watermelons as a bonus. The traditional barbers, as we can see, operate mainly on a barter basis.

The older of the traditional barber brothers in Kafr el-Elow was the official representative of the Helwan Health Department until 1957. In this capacity, he registered newborn babies, granted families permission from the Health Department to bury their dead relatives, and reported any unusual diseases or epidemics. Occasionally, he also administered first aid and practiced folk medicine in the village, although these activities were an illegal extension of his authority. Still another task performed by the older traditional barber was the circumcision of male children, a ritual required by the Islamic religion. (This is discussed further in Chapter 4.)

The older traditional barber in Kafr el-Elow inherited his occupation as barber from his father; he, in turn, passed it on to his younger brother and to his nephew, although the latter received further training in Cairo. The nephew and two other barbers, one from Helwan and one from Cairo, opened barber shops in the village after 1960. They are known as the "modern barbers" because they follow the urban style of haircutting, use modern equipment, and operate strictly on a cash basis, as their customers are primarily young factory workers and students.

THE VILLAGE TAILORS (TARZI) The tailor shop, like the barber shop, is a favorite spot in Kafr el-Elow for villagers to meet regularly, to socialize, and to exchange the latest gossip while drinking tea or coffee. Usually the tailor provides the drinks, but on occasion, one of the regular patrons will bring a pot of tea or coffee from home to share with his friends. The first tailor shop in Kafr el-Elow was established in 1930 by a villager who went to nearby Helwan to learn the trade of making the villagers' native dress, the *jalabiya*. Prior to the late 1940s, when the tailor purchased a second-hand Singer sewing machine, he did all his sewing by hand.

Like the original traditional barber in Kafr el-Elow, the original village tailor passed on his trade to relatives—in this case, to his two sons who help him in the shop. He told me that prior to 1955 his business was very poor because the average *fellah* could not afford to have more than one *jalabiya* made each year. Consequently, he started butchering a sheep once a month and sold the meat to the villagers in order to supplement his income. After the mid fifties, however, his business began to improve as a result of the general upswing in the village economy which accompanied the industrialization of the area, and two more tailors opened shops.

THE VILLAGE BUTCHERS (GAZZAR) Although there are nine butchers in the village, only two operate from locations specifically designated as meat shops. Five have their businesses in front of their homes and two operate at street stands where the meat is suspended from hooks attached to tripods, unprotected from dust, flies, and spoilage. According to government regulations, butchers are supposed to buy their meat from a slaughterhouse where animals are inspected before being killed and their meat is stamped to certify that it has passed government standards. In practice, however, not all butchers in Kafr el-Elow comply with this

*The village tailor*

regulation; instead, they kill their own animals at home according to long-established techniques. Several informants told me that two butchers' businesses had been closed by the government for violating the law. The fact that government inspectors cannot control law violators whose meat business is not transacted at a public shop or street stand helps to explain why five of the nine village butchers have home-based operations.

As in Egypt generally, selling meat is not a daily occupation in Kafr el-Elow. Instead, meat is sold only three or four days each week: Thursday through Sunday. The majority of the butchers slaughter animals—mostly lambs and sheep—on Thursday and Friday mornings, and any meat not sold by Friday evening is sold on Saturday. Since there is no refrigeration in the village, butchers are anxious to dispose of their meat as quickly as possible. Consequently, they sell meat on both cash and credit bases. Essentially, the butchering occupation has not undergone much change in recent years, except for the fact that more meat is butchered and sold due to the increased purchasing power of the villagers.

*A group of villagers sitting in front of the tailor shop*

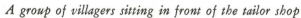

CIVIL SERVICE OCCUPATIONS  The few villagers in Kafr el-Elow who are employed as government workers in Helwan and Cairo can be easily distinguished by their western-style suits as they wait for the bus each morning, and by their packages bearing the names of big city shops as they return home in the late afternoon or early evening. However, these civil servants become an indistinguishable part of the urban scene during the day, and after work they become an equally indistinguishable part of the village setting, removing their modern clothing and donning the traditional *jalabiya*.

TRADITIONAL COMMERCIAL ACTIVITY AT THE WEEKLY MARKET (SUQ) One center of commercial activity in Kafr el-Elow which has not lost its popularity, in spite of the establishment since 1950 of a considerable number of new business establishments in the village, is the weekly market (*suq*). From 1925 until 1955, Sunday was designated as the weekly market day throughout Egypt as this was the official weekly holiday; in 1955, however, Friday became, by government proclamation, the weekly day of rest. Since 1955 Kafr el-Elow, which serves as the market center for several neighboring villages, holds its weekly market every Friday from 6 A.M. until noon, when most men go to the mosque to participate in the Friday-noon prayers. Always regarded as a festive occasion, market day in Kafr el-Elow is a time when the village becomes a place bustling with people and activity. In addition to the peasants from Kafr el-Elow and the surrounding rural areas, urbanites wearing western-style clothing come from the nearby Iron and Steel Company housing project and even from Helwan to buy agricultural products at the market. Thus, market day affords an opportunity for social interaction between villagers and urbanites, as well as between villagers from different areas; while many men, women, and children come to buy, others come simply to "look around" and/or to socialize with friends and relatives.

Most of the merchants participating in the weekly market are itinerants who move from one village to another throughout the year, selling their merchan-

*Religious shaik reciting the Koran in front of the tailor shop*

*Village butcher*

dise on the day or days specifically designated for market activity in each place. Some merchants take their merchandise to market in a wooden wagon which is pulled by a donkey or pushed manually, while others load their goods on a donkey or carry it themselves. Female merchants, who typically sell chickens, geese, pigeons, ducks, and turkeys, usually occupy one side of the market located at the southern entrance to the village. Male merchants occupy another side, and usually sell larger farm animals, such as goats, sheep, donkeys, and calves; grains, such as wheat, barley, and corn; vegetables, such as beans and peas; and agricultural by-products, such as candy, sugar-cane juice, spices, and ingredients used in the preparation of folk medicines. In the center of the market are merchants selling a variety of dry goods, such as fabrics, veils, kitchen utensils, earthenware, glassware, women's jewelry, plastic slippers, mirrors, combs, and handkerchiefs.

The purchasing power of the weekly market's patrons has been greatly enhanced by industrialization, as many now supplement their farm incomes with wages from factory employment. This is reflected not only in the greater variety of products displayed in recent years by the vendors at the weekly market, but also in the increased demand for fresh vegetables and poultry, especially from newcomers in the village who came to Kafr el-Elow specifically to work in the surrounding industries. While most of the market day business today is transacted on a monetary basis, some villagers still purchase on a barter basis, exchanging corn, eggs, and poultry for other commodities.

## MODERN COMMERCIAL ACTIVITY

Since 1950, fifty-nine new businesses have been opened in Kafr el-Elow, several of them rendering services and selling products which were previously un-

*Canal and vendors' carts at weekly market*

obtainable in the village. The six hardware stores, the two electrical supply dealers, the two radio shops, the two shoe repair shops, the two sandwich shops, and the bakery, for example, are types of business which never existed in Kafr el-Elow before 1950, and show very clearly the new patterns of behavior that have appeared in the village as a consequence of industrialization and urbanization. The large number of bachelors among the new industrial workers in the village is reflected by the bakery and sandwich shops; the increasing amount of residential construction discussed in Chapter 1 is reflected by the hardware and electrical supply dealers; the introduction of modern communication facilities is exhibited in the radio shops; and the influence of urban modes of dress, such as wearing shoes, is apparent in the shoe repair shops. These new businesses are modern not only in the sense of being expressions of industrialization and urbanization, but also in the sense of being conducted on a fixed-price, cash-only basis, and situated in a shop rather than in a home setting. In other words, they resemble in most ways similar businesses in Helwan and Cairo.

The Egyptian government has established fixed prices for many basic commodities, such as meat, flour, sugar, and tea, whether sold by traditional or modern merchants, and prosecutes anyone who sells above these prices. Despite this fact, exploitation of consumers, especially long-time residents of the village, is not an uncommon practice in Kafr el-Elow. Merchants are less prone to overcharge strangers or newcomers, since these might be government inspectors or persons who would not be reluctant to report the case to government officials because, they lack, as yet, any close ties with merchants in the village.

### CHANNELS OF OCCUPATIONAL AND COMMERCIAL ACTIVITY

SHOPS  Most of the village shops have come into existence only during the last decade. About 40 percent of them are both owned and operated by families whose members take turns serving the customers. For example, while the husband is working at a factory, his father, wife, or son may "mind the store." In the other 60 percent of the cases, the owner makes a full-time occupation of managing and operating the shop. Goods are sold and services rendered on both cash and credit terms, charge customers paying their accounts on either a monthly or a biweekly basis. Factory workers, who are paid every two weeks, prefer the biweekly payment plan, while civil service employees, who are paid at the end of each month, prefer the monthly payment plan.

VENDORS  At the time I was in Kafr el-Elow, there were only seven vendors' stands in the village, all of them operated by women and specializing in fruits, vegetables, and poultry. Many of these stands are located in front of the vendors' homes. Vendors are especially prominent on market day, which is described earlier in this chapter.

PEDDLERS  Peddlers are itinerant merchants who come to Kafr el-Elow carrying their merchandise in a basket or box, or leading donkey with the merchandise packed on its back or in a cart. They attract customers by shouting for people to "come out and buy." Peddlers sell a wide variety of merchandise, including clothing, yard goods, cosmetics, candy and other sweets, fruits and vegetables. Some even sell on credit—especially yard goods—and collect from their customers when they return to the village. Like street vendors, peddlers are especially prominent at the weekly market in Kafr el-Elow.

*A group of village children posing for a picture*

# 3

# Family and Kinship Organization

KINSHIP ORGANIZATION in Kafr el-Elow is characterized by four components: patrilineal descent, patrilocal residence, patriarchal authority, and preferred kin group endogamy. A considerable range of terminology is used by different writers referring to various family units in the Arab Middle East. The term *bait*, for example, has been used to refer to the smallest family unit, the nuclear family, as well as to a lineage; the term *aila* has been used to refer in different cases, to both a joint family and a lineage and to both immediate and distant relatives. Similarly, the term *ahl* has been used to refer to a person's immediate family or to his entire clan. Because there are no generally applicable terms in the Arabic language to refer to specific family units, the terms used by different writers must be interpreted within a particular context (Murphy and Kasdan 1959:18–19; Evans-Pritchard 1949:75; Gulick 1955:108–109).

Therefore, when referring to various family units, for the sake of clarity I will use terms employed by the villagers in Kafr el-Elow and note their anthropological equivalents, as illustrated in Table 9.

TABLE 9
FAMILY UNIT TERMINOLOGY

| Villagers' Terms | Author's Terms (Anthropological) |
|---|---|
| *hamula* | clan |
| *il aila il kabeera* | lineage |
| *aila* | joint family |
| *bait* | nuclear family |
| *haush* | household |

The relationship between these several levels of family extension may be diagrammed as follows:

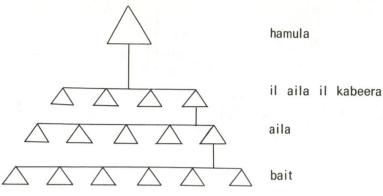

*Figure 11. Genealogy of a Hamula*

A *hamula* (clan), which gradually evolves from a single *bait* (nuclear family), embraces all the levels of family extension below it.

## Family Structure in Kafr el-Elow

When the village of Kafr el-Elow was established nearly 200 years ago, its entire population consisted of only six *ailaat* (plural form of *aila*) or joint families. Today, however, all four levels of family extension illustrated by Figure 11 are represented in Kafr el-Elow. The smallest and least important family unit, from both an economic and social viewpoint, is the *bait* (nuclear family), consisting of a husband and wife and their unmarried offspring. There are three types of *bait* in Kafr el-Elow: (1) the independent nuclear family of recent arrival in the village; (2) the nuclear family belonging to an extended family household; and (3) the nuclear family in its own household, which results from division of the joint extended family upon the death of the father. Independent nuclear families are found exclusively among the recently-arrived factory workers in Kafr el-Elow.

The nuclear family is usually part of, and subordinate to, a second and more complex family unit known as the *aila* (joint family), which consists of a husband and wife, their unmarried *and* married sons, their unmarried and divorced daughters, and any unmarried or divorced paternal aunts. At the head of the *aila* is the grandfather or, if he is deceased, the father. Traditionally, all members of a particular *aila* reside within the same *haush* (household), but each married son's nuclear family occupies a separate residential unit therein.

All the sons of the *aila,* both married and unmarried, are expected to contribute to its financial support, the father or grandfather stipulating the amount from each, usually depending on the size of the son's or grandson's earnings. For example, if one son earns twelve Egyptian pounds per month, his contribution might be set at four to five Egyptian pounds per month, the remainder being saved for him to get married, or, if he is already married, to spend exclusively on himself, his wife and children, or to save. Nevertheless, if a son fails, for one reason or another, to contribute to the *aila*'s financial resources, he does not suffer expulsion from the family unit. Upon the father's death, the *aila* is usually dissolved, the inheritance is divided among the sons, and each of the constituent nuclear families becomes the nucleus of a new *aila*. In other words, a constant cycle from nuclear to joint family and from joint family to nuclear families may be observed.

The *aila* is part of, and subordinate to, a still more complex family unit: *il aila il kabeera* (lineage). This third level of family extension may include five or more direct-line and collateral generations. Since the members of the *il aila il kabeera* do not reside in one household, as do the members of the *aila*, their relationships have greater social than economic significance. Each lineage has a head, referred to as *kabeer il aila* (the elder of the lineage), who speaks for the entire group, represents them at social events, and advises them on important matters.

The fourth level of family extension in Kafr el-Elow is the *hamula* (clan), which embraces all the lineages descended from a common ancestor. According to several elderly informants in Kafr el-Elow, until recently there were six clans in the village, varying in size and generational depth. There are many families in Kafr el-Elow, however, that have not been established in the village long enough to attain the generational depth required to form a *hamula*. The leader of a *hamula*, who is referred to as a *shaik* and whose position is usually hereditary, is expected to resolve disputes between members of his clan and to offer them hospitality when they visit his house.

As one can readily conclude from the preceding discussion of family organization in Kafr el-Elow, kinship ties are not limited to the nuclear family; on the contrary, they are extensive, producing a network of special relations between relatives that makes the kinship group a clearly distinguishable unit within the community. Many elderly informants, when discussing the historical background of the village, not only expressed pride in their immediate relatives but also showed a strong interest in their ability to establish a connection between themselves and a larger kinship group. The number of persons constituting one's *hamula* has always been, and still is, a source of pride in the village, as it is in all rural areas of the Middle East.

## Kinship Terminology

Linguistically, kinship terminology reflects kinship status which, in turn, determines the pattern of interaction among individuals. The kinship terminology used in Kafr el-Elow is basically the same as that used in the Arab world generally, but the pronunciation of certain terms is unique by reason of the dialect peculiar to its region. Figure 12 illustrates kinship terminology used within two ascending and two descending generations, and Figure 13 provides affinal terminology.

Starting with the "ego" or the individual, the clan or lineage name is used for identification purposes. For example, if Ibrahim Abed Il-Atti Saloum's wife gives birth to a baby boy who is named Ahmad, the child will be called Ahmad Ibrahim Abed Il-Atti Saloum, the name Saloum being the *hamula* name, Il-Atti the lineage name, and Ibrahim the father's name. Several other names may also be included, such as that of the paternal grandfather or great-grandfather. Frequently, however, either the lineage or the *hamula* name will be dropped in common usage

2nd ascending generation

| | |
|---|---|
| jiddi | —my grandfather |
| jidati | —my grandmother |

1st ascending generation

| khali | —my mother's brother |
|---|---|
| khalti | —my mother's sister |

| abuya | —my father |
|---|---|
| ummi | —my mother |
| ammi | —my father's brother |
| ammti | —my father's sister |

Ego's generation

| ibn khali | —my mother's brother's son |
|---|---|
| bint khali | —my mother's brother's daughter |
| ibn khalti | —my mother's sister's son |
| bint khalti | —my mother's sister's daughter |

| akhuya | —my brother |
|---|---|
| ukhti | —my sister |
| ibn ammi | —my father's brother's son |
| bint ammi | —my father's brother's daughter |
| ibn ammti | —my father's sister's son |
| bint ammti | —my father's sister's daughter |

EGO

1st descending generation

| ibn ukhti | —my sister's son |
|---|---|
| bint ukhti | —my sister's daughter |

| ibni | —my son |
|---|---|
| awlaadi | —my sons |
| binti | —my daughter |
| banaati | —my daughters |

2nd descending generation

| ibn ibni | —my son's son |
|---|---|
| bint ibni | —my son's daughter |
| ibin binti | —my daughter's son |
| bint binti | —my daughter's daughter |

Figure 12. Kinship Terminology

*mirat ammi* —my father's brother's wife
*zoug ammati* —my father's sister's husband

*mirati* —my wife
*mirat akhuya* —my brother's wife

*mirat khali* —my mother's brother's wife
*zoug khalti* —my mother's sister's husband

*zoug ukti* —my sister's husband

| | |
|---|---|
| | EGO |

*mirat ibni*—my son's wife
*zougbinti* —my daughter's husband

*Figure 13. Affinal Terminology*

for the sake of brevity, so that in the above case the child would be called either Ahmad Ibrahim Saloum or Ahmad Ibrahim Abed Il-Atti. If one's lineage is large, wealthy, and socially prominent within a *hamula*, the lineage name will usually be retained. For official purposes, however, a person always uses his or her complete name.

If an individual is the eldest son, his first name will be used by friends and relatives in referring informally to his father and mother. For example, if Ibrahim's oldest son's name is Ahmad, then Ibrahim may be called Abou Ahmad: the father of Ahmad. A mother may also be referred to by the name of her oldest son; in other words, Ibrahim's wife may be designated as Umm Ahmad. This practice is referred to as teknonymy. Even in cases where a name is merely given in advance to the hoped-for first son of a newly-married couple, friends and relatives may refer to the potential father and mother as *abou* . . . (father of . . .) and *umm* . . . (mother of . . .), respectively. Frequently, a deceased grandfather's name is given to the prospective son, continuing the connection with other members of the kinship group. I discovered, however, that some mothers and fathers in the village were referred to by the name of a younger son who was well-educated or successful rather than by the name of their eldest son. This action has become more prevalent recently as the villagers have become more status-conscious, but the number of parents to whom it applies is still extremely small. I was aware of only three families in Kafr el-Elow who adopted the practice.

Kinship terminology also differentiates an individual's relationship to his paternal from that with his maternal relatives, and distinguishes his first cousins from those more distantly related. For example, when a man refers to his first paternal cousin, he uses the term *ibn-ammi* (my father's brother's son), whereas when he refers to his second paternal cousin, he uses the term *ibn ibn ammi* (my father's brother's son's son). Similarly, when a man refers to his first maternal cousin, he uses the term *ibn khali* (my mother's brother's son), whereas when he refers to his second maternal cousin, he uses the term *ibn ibn khali* (my mother's brother's son's son).

A daughter-in-law may, as a sign of respect, use the term *ammi* to refer to her father-in-law and the term *mirat ammi* to refer to her mother-in-law, even if she is not her husband's father's brother's daughter. Similarly, as an expression of affection, a father-in-law may use the term *ya binti* (my daughter) to address his daughter-in-law, even if she is not his brother's daughter. The terms *hama* and *hamah* may also be used by a daughter-in-law to refer to her husband's father and mother, respectively, and the terms *nasseeb* and *kinna* may be used by parents to refer to a daughter's husband and to a son's wife, respectively.

When collective reference is made to one's kin within five generations, the term *ahl il-lazam* (immediate relatives) is commonly used, but when the term *ahl* is used alone, it refers to all of one's kin. Similarly, while the term *jiddi* refers to both maternal and paternal grandfathers and the term *jidditi* refers to both maternal and paternal grandmothers, a paternal grandfather is specified as *jiddi abu abuya*, and a maternal grandfather as *jiddi abu ummi*. The term for a paternal grandmother is *jidditi umm abuya*, and that for a maternal grandmother is *jidditi umm ummi*.

Finally, age being a very important factor determining the status of an individual in Kafr el-Elow, a person refers collectively to paternal relatives who are older than he as *il-amam* (plural form of *amm*): paternal uncles; those who are younger are called *awlad il-amam*: paternal cousins. Maternal relatives older than a speaker are referred to collectively by the term *akhwal* (singular *khal*): maternal uncles; those who are younger are referred to as *awlad il-akhwal*: maternal cousins.

## Kinship Roles

In Kafr el-Elow, greater importance is placed upon paternal than upon maternal relatives, although they may both belong to the same lineage or *hamula* due to the prevalence of endogamous marriage in the village. If the maternal relatives are members of a different lineage or *hamula*, their subordinate position relative to the paternal relatives is even more conspicuous. This phenomenon is reflected in a proverb well known throughout the Arab Middle East—*il-khal imkhala wa-il-amm moowala*—the literal meaning of which is that after the father, the paternal uncle is the custodian of his nephews and nieces, rather than the maternal uncle. If a feud develops between paternal and maternal relatives, children are expected to identify with and support the former's cause. Nevertheless, children frequently have a strong attachment to their maternal uncles and aunts.

A married woman resides in her spouse's family home, where she plays a role subordinate to both her husband and mother-in-law. Indeed, a husband frequently sides with his mother against his wife. Romantic love between husbands and wives is practically non-existent except among better-educated couples, and even these never demonstrate affection toward one another in the presence of their children. Sexual activity is geared mainly to the husband's satisfaction. The man is unquestionably the head of the household and, as such, his authority is undisputed.

A wife with grown sons still plays a role subordinate to her husband, but she exercises considerable authority in rearing her children and in supervising the household activities of her sons' wives. Conflict frequently occurs if a mother-in-law shows partiality toward one or other of her sons' wives. The wife of a son who occupies a dominant position relative to his brothers by virtue of his superior education or greater financial contributions to the maintenance of the household, or the daughter-in-law who bears the largest number of sons, is very frequently the object of privileged treatment by a mother-in-law. Hamady (1960:39) and Berger (1962:131–134) point out that this pattern is prevalent in Arab countries.

When a wife in Kafr el-Elow is angry with her husband for some reason, she may complain to her father-in-law or to her mother-in-law, the former usually being more sympathetic with her and more willing to criticize his son. In some cases, however, an angry wife may leave her husband's house and go to live with her father or brother until her husband sends a member of his family—his father, uncle, or a close relative—to mediate for her return. Wives who resort to the latter procedure are referred to as *hardana*.

In the village of Kafr el-Elow and throughout Arab countries, fathers guide and discipline their sons while mothers perform the same function for their daughters. Nevertheless, the fact that mothers frequently intervene to temper their husbands' disciplinary action against their sons and that fathers exercise a similarly protective influence with respect to their daughters helps to explain why boys tend to be closer emotionally to their mothers than to their fathers, and girls closer to their fathers than to their mothers, even though these feelings may not be overtly expressed. H. Ammar has expressed the importance, in all Muslim communities of the Middle East, that is placed upon children's obedience to both parents:

> The authority of the parents is sanctioned by the Koran. Obedience of children to their parents comes next to the Moslems' major obligations to God and the Prophet. Disobedience to parents *hokouk al walidain* is one of the major sins which is harshly punished in the next world, and, according to Ali, even in this world. A disobedient son or daughter will never live a successful or happy life on earth, and the parents' curse might even affect the son's or daughter's children. To obtain the parental blessing is more important than to inherit land or wealth from them, as having their blessing is a prerequisite for both piety and success. Thus, if the father is to wield authority and provide protection, the son or daughter must show "filial piety" and submission to him as well as to the mother. (Ammar 1966:52)

In general, however, Arab children of both sexes feel deeply loved at home, in some cases are spoiled, not only by their parents, but also by grandparents, uncles, and aunts on both sides of the family. Paternal grandparents, in particular, tend to favor the children and to give them protection and refuge when their parents try to exercise discipline; it should be noted that their feelings are stronger for their son's male offspring than for either their sons' female offspring or their daughters' offspring (of both sexes). This phenomenon is expressed in the well-known Arabic proverb frequently recited to me by several grandfathers in the village of Kafr el-Elow: "Take care of your son's son and not of your daughter's son" (*rabi ibn ibnak wa ibn bintak la*). The rationale for this statement lies in the fact that the son's son not only perpetuates his father's family name, but is required to care for his paternal grandparents. That the daughter's son does not have a similar responsibility for his maternal grandparents reflects the greater strength of patrilineal than of matrilineal ties in the village.

Throughout his lifetime, a person is expected to accord courtesy and respect not only to his parents, but also to all older members of his *hamula*. In family gatherings he must play a subordinate role, socially and otherwise, to all older persons present, serving them food and giving them seats ahead of himself and all other younger members. It is also considered disrespectful for a younger person to smoke in front of his parents and older relatives, even if they know that he does so and state explicitly that they do not object to his smoking in their presence. This was well illustrated by the following case. An elementary school teacher in the village, a married man in his late twenties who was educated at the Teacher Training Institute in Cairo, was smoking a cigarette during an informal conversation with me in the guest room of his home. However, this cigarette was discarded when his elder brother, a farmer, entered the room. When I questioned him about this behavior after his brother had left, he said he would have reacted in the same manner had his father or an older relative entered the room, because it is an insult to the superior social status of one's elders to smoke in their presence.

Still another example of the importance of age is the fact that the oldest son often becomes temporary master of the household during his father's absence. Even when the father is at home, he frequently consults with his oldest son on various matters. The eldest son's prominent position in the family derives from the fact that he is the first sibling to help his father in the fields or to contribute his earnings from some other occupation to the family income. His younger siblings remain subordinate to him throughout his lifetime; it is his responsibility to care for them, even after his father's death. This behavior pattern reflects the traditional authoritarian character of interpersonal relations in rural areas of Arab countries. During the past few years, however, as the result of increasing educational opportunities, the main criterion determining one's status in the family has been shifting from age to education.

Daughters in Kafr el-Elow are expected to obey both their parents and their brothers. At the age of nine or ten, their mothers assign them certain household tasks such as cooking, cleaning, and caring for their younger brothers and sisters. After reaching the age of twelve, girls are not permitted to leave the house except to purchase necessities when no males are at home and can go instead. Walking through the village alone, they are expected to move swiftly and not to let their eyes wander. When accompanied by their fathers or brothers, they are supposed to walk ten to fifteen yards behind them so that strangers will find it difficult to learn their identity. Even in their homes, girls are not allowed to let themselves be seen by visiting strangers.

It has already been mentioned that the *aila*, the most prominent family unit in the village of Kafr el-Elow, is an economic as well as a social unit, and that the sons pool their resources to support the entire household and to buy or build and then maintain a home. Due in part to this cooperation in the financial support of the joint family to which they belong, brothers have a very strong emotional affinity and tend to defend each other, right or wrong, against opponents. While there is a close relationship between sisters before marriage, interaction between them tends to decrease after marriage unless their husbands are close kin.

## The Mate Selection Process

Because few people in Kafr el-Elow marry outside their clans, few choose a mate who is not a resident of the village. Moreover, marriage to a close relative, especially to a paternal first cousin, is generally preferred to that with a more distant kinsman such as a member of one's lineage or clan. It is commonly said in Kafr el-Elow that the prevailing system of paternal cousin marriage protects a woman against village gossip if she passes a certain age without getting married (*bint il-amm sutra*), because, theoretically, a paternal male cousin has priority of access to his paternal female cousin. Should a girl's distant relative or a man from another clan wish to propose marriage, he would usually send a *waseet* (mediator) to find out whether or not she has been promised to her paternal first cousin or whether her paternal first cousin is thinking of marrying her, before pursuing the girl in question. If it is discovered that the girl's father has refused consent to such a parallel-cousin marriage, few other relatives or outsiders will dare to ask for the girl's hand, for a man has the prerogative of marrying his paternal uncle's daughter, regardless of her father's feelings about the matter. This is generally understood throughout the rural areas of Arab countries (Murphy and Kasdan 1959:18).

Another advantage inherent in the parallel-cousin type of marriage is that the wife will usually be extremely cooperative with her husband because he is a close relative. Moreover, the male paternal cousin suffers much less of a financial burden in regard to the bride price and other marriage expenses than does a non-relative. On the other hand, because a woman retains her family name after marriage, and because a woman's male cousins rank in importance immediately below her father and brothers, any shameful act performed by her will also reflect negatively on the cousins. The mate selection process leading to the marriage of parallel cousins is a simple one; the fathers of the prospective bride and groom, who are brothers, merely discuss the matter informally and then set a date for the wedding.

The following pattern of mate selection is pursued by men in the village of Kafr el-Elow who marry outside their own clan. Having observed or heard about a desired girl, a young man tells his mother who, in turn, conveys the happy idea to her husband. If the father agrees to his son's choice, he usually asks his wife to send a *waseet*—most frequently a female neighbor or a relative—to visit the girl's parents to determine whether or not she has already been promised to someone; if not, the person will at this point seek their consent for her marriage to the son. The girl's father is the principal decision-maker in this situation. Depending on his reaction to the proposed son-in-law, he will either tell his wife to reject or to accept the mediator's marriage plan. If the mediator's account is favorable, the boy's mother visits the girl's mother to confirm the report. Following this confirmation, the fathers of the future bride and groom meet to work out the details of the wedding, and both agree to announce the happy event officially, the boy's father paying for all the expenses. The prospective spouses, especially the girl, have very little to say about their marriage plans, and in some cases they are not even consulted. If the prospective bridegroom is employed and able to pay his own marriage expenses, however, the father is less restrictive, both about his son's choice of a mate and about the type of wedding ceremony.

In cases where the prospective spouses are from different villages, the mediation process described above is followed, but if the mediator's report is favorable, both the father and mother of the boy visit the girl's home. On this occasion, the girl will be called upon by her father to prepare and serve tea for her prospective parents-in-law. If she meets their expectations in this regard, as well as in her general appearance and decorum, they will encourage the proposed match subsequent to their visit; if not, they are polite and sociable while at her home, but consider the case closed upon leaving. An extremely important characteristic of a mediator's role in arranging marriages is confidentiality, especially in cases where negotiations break down, because most villagers are deeply concerned about saving face before their friends and relatives.

## Pre-Nuptial Rituals

On the date agreed upon by the fathers of the prospective spouses as the engagement day (*youm il-shabka*), the groom's parents and a small group of their closest relatives take presents to the future bride's home. The variety and value of the gifts reflect the socioeconomic position of the prospective groom's family. Some characteristic items presented to future brides by their prospective female in-laws are one or two pieces of dressmaking material, a piece of jewelry—usually a gold bracelet or a necklace—and two wedding rings. On their way to the future bride's home, the mother of the prospective groom and the female relatives sing and utter various cries of joy (*zagareet*). The future groom's father also sends gifts—usually meat, rice, vegetables, and soft drinks—to the prospective bride's home on the engagement day.

After both families (including the prospective couple) and their guests have eaten a meal together, the father of the future groom thanks the prospective bride's father for his hospitality and goes through the formality of publicly asking for his daughter's hand in marriage by saying, "We will be honored if we get closer to you" (*ihna talbeen il gurb*). The prospective bride's father replies by saying, *gurbukum sharaf*, which means the honor is his and that his future in-laws' visit to his home has not been in vain. Then he shakes hands with the prospective groom and his father. Next, the future groom puts a wedding ring on his bride's as well as on his own finger—a relatively recent custom—while his father makes a portion of the marriage payment (*mahr*), referred to as *mugaddam* (in advance), to the bride's father. Because the remainder, called the *muakhar* (the delayed), is payable only in case of divorce and death, it operates as a kind of security measure discouraging the husband from dismissing his wife in the future. The future bride's father uses most of the *mugaddam* portion of the *mahr* to buy furniture for his daughter and to cover the wedding expenses; the remainder goes into his own pocket as compensation for losing his daughter. In certain cases, both fathers agree to buy the basic furniture needed by the couple, and in still other cases the groom buys all the furniture.

In Kafr el-Elow the total *mahr* usually varies in amount from 50 to 400 Egyptian pounds, depending on what the couple's parents agree upon. In paternal first-cousin marriages, the fathers of the prospective bride and groom do not always agree on any specific *mahr*, operating on the assumption that both will voluntarily purchase whatever the couple needs and desires without having to be bound by a formal contract. However, since Islam requires the payment of a *mahr*, though not any specific amount, the fathers frequently agree to specify in the marriage contract a *mahr* of one pound. This is done simply to comply with the prescription of the Koran, in spite of the fact that marriage is generally regarded as a secular rather than a religious affair. The small amount reflects the strong affectional bond between brothers which motivates them to avoid the possibility of financially exploiting one another. In a few instances, when a father wishes to discourage his daughter's marriage to her paternal first cousin, he may demand such an enormous *mahr* from the boy's father—as much as 1000 Egyptian pounds—that even if he were a wealthy man the sum would be considered outrageous and the proposed marriage not worth the price.

During the engagement day the fathers of the prospective couple also agree upon the time for signing the marriage contract, referred to as *katib il-kitab*. On the appointed date, the legal representative of the bride and groom and two witnesses sign the marriage contract in the presence of the marriage registrar (*mazun*), who finally affixes his own signature as well. While Egyptian law specifies a minimum marriage age of sixteen years for girls and eighteen years for boys, the *mazun* often ignores this requirement, especially if he is paid well for his services.

Islam also specifies that the girl should be asked to give her consent to the marriage, but this, too, is seldom done in the village. When the ritual of signing the marriage contract has been completed, the entire group which is assembled for the occasion at the bride's home recites the opening chapter of the Koran (*Fatiha*). While the couple is legally married after the signing of the marriage contract, the wedding ceremony itself does not take place until several days or even several months later, on a date selected, again, by the couple's fathers. During the period between the engagement and the wedding day, on holidays such as *Eid-il-Adha* or *Eid il-Fitr* the family of the groom usually sends his bride gifts such as meat, rice, and holiday cookies. If they are wealthy, they may also send her a piece of material and some jewelry.

A few days before the wedding (*lailat iddukhla*), the groom and his brother or one of his male cousins go around the village inviting their kinsmen and friends to the event. The night preceding the wedding (*lailat il-henna*), both the bride and groom celebrate with their friends in their respective homes. At the groom's home, the village barber rubs the hands and feet of the groom with *henna*, and some of the guests do the same. Soft drinks (*sharbat*) and tea are then served while the groom's friends sing and dance. His mother, sisters, and female relatives celebrate in a similar manner, but in a different part of the house. This prenuptial social affair usually lasts late into the evening. The party at the bride's home is identical, for all practical purposes. The day preceding the wedding is also the occasion for the bride's parents to carry her new furniture and personal possessions to the groom's home, where both families arrange the items in the room reserved for the newlywed couple.

## The Wedding Day (*Youm iddukhla*)

On the wedding day itself, the bride and groom participate in still another ritual; the groom undergoes a haircutting and bathing ceremony, and the bride experiences a bathing and beautifying ceremony. The groom is usually invited during the previous night's prenuptial party to hold this ritual at the home of one of his friends. In addition, all of the men present the night before are invited to attend the haircutting and bathing ceremony. The village barber not only cuts the hair of the prospective groom, but that of any guests who so desire. The host warms the water for the groom's bath, but the barber actually bathes him, some of the groom's friends pinching and patting his shoulders, symbolizing their desire to undergo the same ceremony themselves in the not-too-distant future. Others sing, dance, and clap, as do some females standing outside the bathing chamber. After the groom is bathed, he is helped to dress and then seated on a chair surrounded by his friends, who sing praises to him and to their host. During the singing, they give monetary donations (*nkout*) to the barber as compensation for his contribution to the wedding ceremonies. He, in turn, commends them for loving and honoring the groom and specifies the amount each has donated, which usually varies from three to fifteen piasters. In the meantime, the host serves soft drinks and tea to the guests.

When the groom leaves his friend's home after the haircutting and bathing ceremony, he walks in a procession to his parents' home, flanked by two friends who serve as body guards. A *baladi* (rural) band from a neighboring village, consisting of a flutist, a tambourinist, and a drummer, usually leads the procession, the musicians receiving from most people a monetary donation. Some of the groom's young relatives follow the procession, singing, clapping, and beating the *tabla* (a small drum). As the procession moves slowly through the village, it stops several times in front of various shops, where the leader of the band shouts and sings out an invitation for the people to come and honor the groom. Women of the village usually go to the roofs of their homes to watch the procession. Close friends and relatives of the groom may throw salt from their rooftops to drive away the evil eye from those walking in the procession.

When the procession reaches the groom's home, the participants enter a  big tent (*sewan*) rented especially for the wedding, wherein they sit on chairs or on mats while eating and being entertained by the musicians. Meanwhile, the barber stands beside the groom and greets the male guests, many of whom offer *nkout*. The barber thanks each donor individually, and a relative of the groom records the amount of money received so that, in the future, when that person or one of his sons gets married, the *nkout* can be returned in the same amount or more. Indeed, some of the guests who give money to the groom at any given wedding are repaying what they were given by the father of the groom when they were married. Those who fail to reciprocate in this manner receive a note by messenger reminding them of their obligation. Failure to heed the notice would be considered a grave insult to the groom and his family. The groom's close relatives usually send their donations to him two or three days before the wedding; and rice, sugar, tea, or a live sheep or goat are customary gifts. Kinsmen who prefer to make their donations in the form of money, however, do so on the wedding day itself, along with friends of the groom.

The bride's bathing and beautification rites usually take place at her own home and are conducted by a *ballana* (one who prepares brides for weddings), who uses a piece of wet, red material to rub the bride's face so that it will look rosy. In recent years, commercial rouge has frequently been used for this purpose. Female friends who attend the ceremony sing, clap, and entertain the bride while her family serves soft drinks and tea. After the bride has been physically prepared for her wedding, the groom's family comes to take her and her family to their home. If the distance between the two homes is short, they walk in procession, singing and dancing. When walking is not feasible because the bride comes from another village, the groom will send a taxi or two to bring her and her family to his home. Some of the writer's elderly informants in Kafr el-Elow commented that they preferred the old way of transporting the bride and her family on the wedding day;

that is by providing them with a camel and parading them around the village before the ceremony. This practice was discontinued in the late 1940s because of the rise of industrialization and the accompanying modernization of the village.

When the bride reaches the groom's home, she is seated on a platform so that she can be readily seen by all the female guests in the room and in the courtyard. The groom visits her briefly after her arrival, but then leaves to join his male guests who are seated in a different room or house, or in the tent erected outside his home for the occasion. While the bride is on display, females who have been invited to the wedding entertain her until late in the evening by singing, clapping, and dancing to the beat of the tambourine. Food, soft drinks, and tea are served to the bride and her guests during this entertainment. Later, the bride's female guests view her new clothing and furniture, the amount and quality of which tend to reflect the groom's social status, inasmuch as his family purchases these items. The bride also shows her guests the chest of goods supplied by her own family, for it is customary in the village for mothers to save money earned from the sale of poultry and poultry products in order to buy their daughters jewelry, clothing, and cooking utensils in anticipation of their wedding day. Village women gossip for many months about the gifts they have seen on a bride's wedding day.

The wedding ceremony itself is a joyous event, not only for the couple united in marriage, but for their relatives as well. The lavishness of the event depends, of course, on the socio-economic position of the families involved. The following is an account of a wedding ceremony in the village to which I was invited. Mr. B was a wealthy and prominent man[1] who owned a truck with which he transported cement for the village cement factory to various construction projects in the Helwan area. His seventeen-year-old son, who was employed as a laborer in a textile factory near the village, had a reputation of being a playboy, spending most of his earnings, as well as money he took from his mother, on girls in Cairo. Consequently, his mother and father decided that it would be good for him to assume the responsibilities of marriage, and they chose for his future wife a fifteen-year-old paternal cousin who lived next door. Mr. B proposed his idea to his brother, who gave his consent to the marriage, and both fathers agreed on a wedding date. While the young man and woman were informed of their fathers' decision, the issue was not a matter for disagreement.

Soon thereafter, both fathers requested the services of a *mazun* to assist them in executing the marriage contract. Both fathers lied to the *mazun* about the girl's age, since at fifteen she was one year under the marriage age established by Egyptian civil law. After the *mahr* was specified and the contract was written and signed by both fathers, two witnesses, and the *mazun*, the wedding date was set for a month later. In the meantime, the fathers purchased a bedroom suite for the prospective married couple and placed it in the room designated for the newlyweds at the groom's house. This was considered an exceptional case by village standards, for very few families, it seems, possessed a bedroom suite. One week before the wedding, the groom and his brother went about the village personally inviting people to attend the ceremony.

---

[1] The man in this case has been designated as Mr. B for the sake of confidentiality. Mr. B was wealthy only in terms of village standards.

Although the groom had his hair cut in Helwan early on his wedding day, he also underwent the traditional haircutting and bathing ceremony later that day in Kafr el-Elow. Rumors circulated that the bride had also gone to Helwan on her wedding day to have her hair set at a beauty shop. This was an unconventional thing for her to do because professional beauty care has been traditionally regarded as degrading to a woman's morals, although many young women in the village express a desire to avail themselves of such services.

Following the groom's haircutting and bathing ceremony, the wedding procession began, led by a group of local musicians. When the procession reached the front of the groom's home, a photographer from Helwan took the groom's picture with some of his friends. The photographer later took a picture of the bride and groom inside the house. I was told this was the first time in the history of the village that a professional photographer had been hired to take pictures of a wedding.

After the pictures had been taken, the wedding guests entered the groom's home for a meal. The female guests ate with the bride in one room, while the male guests ate in another with the groom. Meat from a cow that had been butchered for the occasion was placed on a brass tray and served with a sauce over rice. Following the dinner, the guests were seated by the groom's father in a *sewan* which had been set up outside the house for the wedding festivities. Placement of the guests was according to social rank. My research assistant and I, four prominent villagers as well as the police captain, and three of his secret agents, sat together in one corner of the *sewan*.

Soon the male guests were entertained by a group of musicians imported from Cairo for the occasion at a cost to the groom's father of twenty-five Egyptian pounds. I was informed that musicians had been brought from Cairo for only two or three weddings in the past. The entertainment began with religious songs but then shifted to nationalistic songs in praise of President Nasser's revolutionary achievements. Songs were also sung in recognition of the host's hospitality and in appreciation of the villagers' cordiality. In appreciation of the performance, the villagers donated money to the musicians in amounts ranging from one-half Egyptian pound to one Egyptian pound.

As the entertainment continued, tea and soft drinks were served to the male guests. In addition, certain privileged guests were provided with a *goza* (water pipe), lighted charcoal, and an individually-wrapped cube of hashish. This is a most unusual form of hospitality, not only because hashish smoking is forbidden by Egyptian law, but because it is an extremely expensive practice. One member of each group of special guests mixed the hashish with *muassal* (sweet tobacco) and put it in the funnel-shaped head of the water pipe, covering the mixture with hot charcoal. The water pipe was then passed around to the other members of the group, each taking two or three deep puffs. Some of the special guests drank beer or a heavy and dark sweet tea while smoking the *goza* in order to achieve more quickly the feeling of being high. The hashish-smoking session lasted for about three hours.

The *sahra* (wedding night entertainment) does not usually come to an end until well after midnight, when the groom goes to the newlyweds' room, where his bride has been awaiting his arrival and has prepared some food for him to eat.

The following moments are extremely difficult ones for the couple, especially for the bride, who, in most cases, fears that the first act of sexual intercourse will be painful. The groom may try to conceal his own tensions and appear confident in front of his bride, or attempt to scare her into giving in to him. Some grooms try to minimize their bride's fear of sexual intercourse by being gentle or by bribing her with a gift of one to three pounds. In addition, the bride's mother, sisters, and female relatives usually try to relieve her tension before they leave the groom's home on the wedding night by talking about sex and assuring her that intercourse is not to be feared.

Reports circulate in the village that some grooms slap or beat their brides with a stick if other methods of inducing them to surrender are not successful. Such techniques are gradually disappearing, however, especially among the younger generation who know more about sex and who tend to view marriage more romantically than did previous generations. In the past, it was not uncommon for the bride's father to insist that the groom present him with a handkerchief stained by the blood from the girl's torn hymen as proof of his daughter's virginity, a factor which was supposed to considerably enhance the honor of the girl and her family. The following verses, still sung by the families of some young men on the day following the wedding, reflect the traditional importance placed upon virginity in the village:

> Oh beautiful bride who has covered the white silk with her blood. Ye stars revolving and shining over her father's house. You beautiful girl with a figure of a date tree who brought honor to your family. Send messengers to inform her father to eat and relax, because the blood of his daughter flows to cover the bed.

Traditionally, the groom broke the bride's hymen by inserting his fingers into her vagina. An elderly woman would frequently witness the event and even assist the groom in breaking the bride's hymen, but this latter practice has almost disappeared over the past ten to fifteen years. When I asked the groom in the wedding described above if he had followed the traditional procedure of showing a blood-stained handkerchief to his bride's father as proof of her virginity, he replied that he had not done so because he considered this to be a ridiculous practice. While such traditional rituals are gradually disappearing, premarital chastity is still expected.

For three consecutive days following the wedding, the bride's mother brings breakfast and dinner to the couple. To the dinners, which usually consist of rice, meat, and bread, the groom invites all or most of his friends who gave him *nkout* on his wedding night.

## Polygyny

Since the residents of Kafr el-Elow are Moslems, any man in the village who so desires may practice polygyny. During the period I was in the village, however, informants told me that there were not more than seven men in the village who were married to more than one woman, and most of these had only two wives.

It is therefore safe to conclude that polygyny is the exception rather than the rule in Kafr el-Elow, and that monogamy is the prevailing or dominant form of marriage. Upon inquiring about the reasons for some men's marrying more than one woman, despite its general unpopularity in the village, I was frequently told that a particular man's first wife could not bear children and that she encouraged her husband to marry another woman. She may even have made the selection herself from among those women with whom she thought she could live harmoniously. In some instances, this resulted in the husband's marriage to his wife's sister (sororate marriage). Another factor offered in explanation for a husband's marrying a second wife was the serious and prolonged illness of his first wife. A third and final reason cited was the desire of wealthy men to demonstrate their high social status by simultaneously supporting two women. While the two wives in all these cases may share the husband and the housework more or less equally and refer to one another as sisters, and the children may call both wives mother, the first wife usually enjoys seniority and receives more respect from the husband, especially if she does not oppose his second wife. If she is the jealous type, however, and strenuously objects to his second wife, her husband may divorce her.

The first wife's family usually opposes her husband's marriage to a second woman, except for the reason of producing children. Moreover, if a man has older children, they often object to his marrying another woman, even if their mother is deceased. This is especially true if any of the man's sons are married, because in this case, the son, his wife, and any unmarried daughters can take care of him. Their opposition might be further motivated by the desire to prevent their father from having more children, who would be a burden for them to supervise and would eventually share in their inheritance.

## Widowhood

That the number and percentage of widows has been consistently greater than the number and percentage of widowers in Kafr el-Elow for several decades is clearly indicated by Table 10.

A major explanation for this discrepancy is that the villagers do not approve of a widow's remarrying after her husband's death, unless she marries her husband's brother (levirate marriage) or a poor man who cannot afford to pay a dowry. The most respectable path for a widow to follow is to remain unmarried and to stay with her deceased husband's family, who will support not only her, but also any children she may have. Other factors contributing to the larger number and percentage of widows than widowers in Kafr el-Elow are the greater life expectancy of women; men's unwillingness to marry women older than themselves, or even of the same age if they are beyond the child-bearing years; men's reluctance to marry a non-virgin or a woman with children, especially if they have children of their own who object to their father's remarriage (the reasons for this are discussed above); and the relative disadvantage of women in taking the initiative in matchmaking, which is complicated by the fact that women's lives are more circumscribed or sheltered than are those of men, limiting their freedom to circulate in public places and their opportunities for meeting men.

TABLE 10
WIDOWED PERSONS IN KAFR EL-ELOW IN SELECTED YEARS

| Year | Widowers | | Widows | | Totals |
|------|------|---------|------|---------|--------|
| | NO. | PERCENT | NO. | PERCENT | |
| 1937 | 21 | 16.7 | 105 | 83.3 | 126 |
| 1947 | 19 | 11.0 | 154 | 89.0 | 173 |
| 1960 | 16 | 5.4 | 280 | 94.6 | 296 |

Source: *U. A. R. Census Book* 1937, 1947, and 1960: pp. 26, 21, and 210, respectively.

## Divorce

Divorce, like polygyny, is regarded in Islam as a male prerogative. More-over, a man may divorce his wife simply by telling her "You are divorced" (*rouhi talka*), without justifying his action to anybody. Islam also provides that, within four months after divorcing his wife, a man may reclaim her without her consent, provided it is only his first or second divorce (Koran, 11:225, 226, and 228) and that at the time he divorced her he did not repeat the words *rouhi talkah bi italata* three times, in which case the divorce would be considered final. A man who de-sires to have this last restriction lifted, however, can easily accomplish this objec-tive by consulting a *mufti* (religious judge), who will usually contrive some *fatwa* (justification) for excepting his client from the general rule. On the other hand, for a wife to obtain a divorce under Islamic law is a difficult task, for she must present her case before *il-mahkama il-shariya*: the Islamic religious court. If a woman's husband agrees to her securing a divorce, however, complications are reduced.

Despite the ease with which men may secure a divorce under Islamic law, a very small percentage of Kafr el-Elow's villagers are divorced, as shown by the statistics in Table 11. Let us examine some of the factors accounting for this low divorce rate. First, since the paternal-cousin type of endogamous marriage pre-dominates in Kafr el-Elow, if a man divorces his wife it means that he is not only divorcing his paternal cousin, for whose general welfare he has responsibility, after her father and brothers, but he is also embarrassing the members of his lineage and clan. As a result, when conflict develops between a husband and wife from the same clan and community, their respective fathers or uncles usually attempt to reconcile the couple as quietly as possible lest gossip further complicate matters and reflect negatively upon the reputation of the entire lineage.

In cases where a husband and wife on the brink of divorce come from dif-ferent clans or communities, the elders of each meet in an effort to reconcile the couple; if they fail, they submit the case to the Arab Council in the village where the couple resides or to the Council in a neighboring community, whose members might be more familiar with the tribal customs and skillful in resolving disputes. If the Arab Council cannot reconcile the couple, after carefully reviewing their sit-uation, the marriage is dissolved.

TABLE 11
MARRIED AND DIVORCED PERSONS IN KAFR EL-ELOW: 1937, 1947 AND 1960

| Year | No. of Divorced Men | No. of Divorced Women | Total No. of Divorced Men and Women | Total No. of Married Men and Women | Percentage Divorced Relative to Total No. Married |
|------|------|------|------|------|------|
| 1937 | 16 | 18 | 34 | 1111 | .030 = 3.0% |
| 1947 | 19 | 19 | 38 | 1696 | .022 = 2.2% |
| 1960 | 17 | 25 | 42 | 2648 | .016 = 1.6% |

Source: *U. A. R. Census Book* 1937, 1947, and 1960: pp. 26, 21, and 210, respectively.

In all divorce actions, the husband is required to pay a specified amount of alimony (*nafaka*) for the support of his children and former wife. If he refuses to comply with the Arab Council's alimony judgment, the civil court forces him to pay by requiring his employer to withhold a certain amount each week from his salary or wages. Such action is rarely necessary in Kafr el-Elow, however; when it is, the husband is usually an employee of one of the factories in the area. If the divorced couple has children, their custody is awarded the mother until sons reach the age of seven and daughters the age of nine; at this time, according to Islamic law, the father assumes custody and child-support payments to the former wife cease.

Islam, by promising a heavenly reward to those who promote reconciliation between discordant husbands and wives, is a second major factor accounting for the low divorce rate in Kafr el-Elow. However, not all efforts at reconciliation are religiously motivated. A wife's father may encourage his daughter to return to her husband in order to avoid having to support her. He may also be interested in obviating the friction which might develop between his daughter and other females in his household, especially his sons' wives, and between their respective children, should she come to live in his home permanently after becoming divorced. A third factor accounting for the low divorce rate in Kafr el-Elow is the husband's reluctance to repay part of his wife's dowry, the amount of which is stated in the marriage contract.

Divorce, in Kafr el-Elow anyway, seems to occur for certain prominent reasons. Village informants told me that disobedience, neglect of duty, and nagging are among the more popular charges. Disobedience might consist of a wife's refusal to wash her husband's clothes; neglect of duty might be a wife's failure to have her husband's meal prepared when he returns from work in the evening because she has been socializing with neighbors or relatives; nagging, finally, could be a wife's persistently urging her husband to spend or borrow more money to satisfy her needs. It should be recognized, however, that authoritarian husbands who are selfish with the family income, who beat their wives during every minor argument, or who are so jealous that they object to their wives' speaking to any other men— even relatives—sometimes provoke their mates into disobedience, irresponsibility, and nagging. Finally, according to village informants, conflict between a wife and her mother-in-law often contributes to divorce, especially when the husband takes his mother's part. As mentioned earlier in this chapter, however, endogamous marriages reduce considerably the possibility of serious conflict developing between a wife and members of her husband's family.

## Social Class

Earlier in this study, I pointed out that landholding and property ownership have been extremely limited in Kafr el-Elow since the village was established. The fact that the total amount of cultivated land in Kafr el-Elow has doubled during the last half-century has not significantly benefited any particular group of villagers, since individual land ownership does not exceed five *feddan*. Indeed, only a few villagers own as many as five *feddan*. Consequently, land ownership, such a prominent factor delineating social classes in most Middle Eastern societies—certainly in Egypt prior to the land reform law of 1952—has never served this function in Kafr el-Elow.

A second factor which has minimized class distinctions in Kafr el-Elow is the strong kinship ties binding the members of each *aila*. For example, when I inquired about class differences between members of each *aila* or between the various *hamula* in the village, informants usually quoted a common Arabic proverb, *ish-how hassanak ani wa-inta ibn ammi,* which means, literally, "What makes you better or of a higher status than I, since you are my cousin or kin?" In other words, the economic success and resulting prestige of one member of an *aila* is shared by all of his kin. If any individual is ranked above his kin, his superior position is based on such personal qualities as generosity (*karam*) or courage (*shahama*). The only real evidence of social class distinction in Kafr el-Elow is the tendency for long-established residents to express a feeling of superiority relative to newcomers in the village by the statement: *sukan il-balad il-asliyiin,* or "We are the original settlers of the village."

While class differences are still virtually nonexistent in the village of Kafr el-Elow, I anticipate that as employment and income opportunities continue to expand, new styles of living and a distinct class system will gradually emerge in the village.

# 4

# Religious Beliefs and Practices

## The Basic Tenets of Islam

THE ADHERENTS OF ISLAM, whether they belong to the *Sunnite* or *Shia* branch of the religion, are extremely reluctant to criticize the Koran, which they believe contains the word of God revealed to the prophet Muhammad through the Angel Gabriel. In addition to the Koran as a guide for daily living, the villagers have the Hadith: a record of the activities and teachings of the prophet Muhammad and his companions. The theology of Islam rests on five pillars—the profession of faith in one God, Allah (*Al-Shahada*); prayer (*As-Salat*); the fast of Ramadan (*As-Saum*); almsgiving (*Az-Zakat*); and pilgrimage to Mecca (*Al-Hajj*)—referred to collectively as *Arkan al-Din* or *Arkan al-Islam*. As devout Muslims, most of the villagers in Kafr el-Elow believe that it is necessary to observe these five practices faithfully in order to gain eternal salvation. The writer will, therefore, deal with each in greater detail.

### *Al-Shahada*—THE PROFESSION OF FAITH

The most important tenet of Islam is that "there is no God but God, and the prophet Muhammad is His messenger" (*La-illaha illa-Allah Wa-Muhammad rasul Allah*). The role of Muhammad in the world is delineated by the Koran as follows:

> Muhammad is the father of no man among you. He is the apostle of Allah and the seal of the prophets. Allah has knowledge of all things. Prophet, we have sent you forth as a witness, a bearer of good news, and a warner; one who shall call men to Allah by his leave and guide them like a shining light. Tell the faithful that Allah has bounteous blessings in store for them. (Koran, 33:40, 45–47)

It is important to point out, however, that Islam regards Muhammad as the last, not the sole, messenger from God serving to recall men to Allah, for both Moses

75

and Jesus are recognized as prophets who came at earlier periods in history to show people (*il-basharia*) the light. Concerning the relationship of faithful Muhammadans to Allah and his prophet, the Koran states:

> Obey Allah and obey the Apostle. If you give no heed to him, know that our apostle's duty is no more than to make plain his message. Allah—there is no God but He. In Allah let the faithful put their trust. (Koran, 4:12–13)

While Muhammadans, like Christians, conceive of their god as indivisible (*wahid*) and present everywhere at all times (*maujoud fii kul makaan*), they reject the Christian belief in the Trinity (three persons in one God) as polytheism (*shirk*), in accordance with the following Koranic injunction:

> They are unbelievers who say "God is the Messiah, Mary's Son." For the Messiah said, "Children of Israel serve God, My Lord and your Lord." Verily, whosoever associates with God anything, God shall prohibit him entrance to paradise, and his refuge shall be the fire; and wrongdoers shall have no helpers. They are unbelievers who say "God is the third of three." No God is there but One God. (Koran, 5:76–78)

When the writer asked the villagers of Kafr el-Elow about their concept of God, the comment was frequently made, especially by elderly persons, that God is merciful (*raheem*), generous (*kareem*), and omnipresent.

### As-Salat—PRAYERS

The second pillar of Islam—prayer—obligates all believers to pray five times daily—alone or in a group, at home, in a mosque, or wherever they happen to be when traveling—and to face eastward (*qibla*)—toward Mecca—while doing so. The five prayer periods are designated as follows: (1) *salat es-subh* (morning prayer), which is to be said before sunrise; (2) *salat al-thur* (noon prayer); (3) *salat al-asr* (afternoon prayers); (4) *salat al-magrib* (evening prayer after sunset); and (5) *salat il-ishaa* (night prayer), which is to be said around 9 P.M. Since the Friday noon prayer period is regarded as the most important of all, devout Muslims make a concerted effort to attend services at a mosque each week at this time. The mosque in Kafr el-Elow is so crowded for the Friday noon prayer service that it is usually necessary for some of the villagers to attend the service in nearby Helwan. In Cairo it is often necessary to place straw mats on the sidewalks in front of mosques to seat those who cannot be accommodated inside. An important feature of the Friday noon prayer service is the sermon (*khot-ba*), given by the *shaik* of the mosque, which may touch upon many different aspects of life. In some instances, the sermon is used for political purposes; that is, to support the governing regime. Several villagers in Kafr el-Elow who are civil service employees in Helwan or Cairo told me that they especially enjoyed attending the Friday noon prayer services in these larger cities because the *shaik's* sermons were more enlightening and sophisticated than those delivered at the mosque in Kafr el-Elow.

Muslims are expected to wash before each of the five prayer periods, as indicated by the following statement from the Koran:

> Believers, when you rise to pray, wash your faces and your hands as far as the elbow, and wipe your heads and your feet to the ankle. If you are polluted, cleanse yourself. But if you are sick or traveling the road; or if, when you have just relieved yourselves or had intercourse with women, you can find no water, take some clean sand and rub your hands and faces with it. Allah does not wish to burden you; he seeks only to purify you and to perfect his favor to you, so that you may give thanks. Remember the favors which Allah has bestowed upon you, and the covenant with which he bound you when you said: "We hear and obey." Have fear of Allah. He knows your innermost thoughts. (Koran, 5:6–7)

Moreover, before every prayer the following introduction to the Koran (*al-Fatiha*) must be recited:

> In the name of Allah, the compassionate, the merciful, praise be to Allah, Lord of the creative, the compassionate, the merciful, King of the last judgment! You alone we worship, and to you alone we pray for help. Guide us to the straight path, the path of those whom you have favored, not those who have incurred your wrath, nor of those who have gone astray. (Koran, 1:1)

I observed that many of the male villagers of Kafr el-Elow were conscientious in their observance of the Friday noon prayer obligation, but very few, especially among the younger generation, prayed five times a day. Yet at noon and in the afternoon, when most of the village men were outside of their homes, many could be seen interrupting their work in the fields, or their conversations inside or in front of various business establishments, to pray. Moreover, elderly persons could be seen praying as they walked about the village or sat on mats in front of their favorite shops: those of the village tailors and barbers.

The questionnaire administered to the residents of Kafr el-Elow supported these observations regarding prayer in the village: only twenty-six percent of the younger respondents indicated that they prayed daily, the remaining seventy-four percent praying less regularly. In contrast with this, older respondents replied almost unanimously that they prayed daily. "Lack of time" was the principal reason offered by the younger respondents for neglecting their daily prayers. Secularism's lesser influence on the older than on the younger generation was also expressed by the former's considering a new mosque the most urgently needed facility in the village, whereas the latter preferred a clinic.

### As-Saum—The Fast of Ramadan

One of the most exacting acts of worship in Islam is the fast of Ramadan, whereby for one month (the ninth) of their lunar calendar each year Muslims assert that man has higher needs than food. The Koran explains the significance of this third pillar of the faith as follows:

> O Believers, prescribed for you is the fast, even as it was prescribed for those that were before you. . . . [This shall be during] the month of "Ramadan," wherein the Koran was sent down to be a guidance to the people and a clear sign of salvation. So let those of you who are present at the month fast it; and if any of you be sick or on a journey, then a number of other days . . . And eat and drink until the white thread shows clearly to you from the black thread at dawn; then complete the fast until the night. (Koran, 11:183–187)

The practice of fasting as a spiritual discipline is both ancient and widespread, antedating Islam. According to the Hadith, for example, prior to his founding the religion of Islam, Muhammad had observed the fast of *Ashura*, a custom derived from the Jewish Day of Atonement; his tribe, the *Quraysh*, had placed special religious significance on the ninth month of the year (Ramadan) as a period of penance. It was during one of his vigils of devotion and penance in the month of Ramadan that Muhammad supposedly received his first revelation from God, thus linking the month of Ramadan with Islam.

The month of Ramadan begins with the report of a new moon by a trustworthy witness, the subsequent thunder of cannon, the calling of the *muezzin* from the mosque minarets and, in modern times, with excited announcements over the radio to alert the people. Reporting the new moon is the responsibility of the religious hierarchy at Al-Azhar University in Cairo. If atmospheric conditions make their observation of the new moon impossible, the length of the preceding month (Shaban), normally twenty-nine days, is extended to thirty days, at the end of which fast becomes obligatory.

While fasting, believers must abstain from all food and drink and must observe strict continence from the break of dawn to sunset. Food is eaten only during the hours of darkness or, as expressed by the Koran, "until the white thread can be clearly distinguished from the black thread at dawn" (Koran, 11:183–187). Any Muslim breaking the fast, with or without an excuse, is expected to make amends (*gada*) for the days of fasting omitted. Even pregnant or nursing women, who usually do not fast consistently, are required to make amends for the days omitted by giving a bushel of wheat to the poor. Each day during the month of Ramadan, as the shadows lengthen and the sun is about to set behind the horizon, *muezzin* climb minarets to call believers to evening prayer and to the breaking of the fast. At the exact moment the sun sinks behind the horizon, the call is punctuated by the firing of a cannon, an innovation introduced during the period of the Ottoman Empire. The radio has also been employed in recent times to announce the end of the daily fast.

During Ramadan, activity in the village of Kafr el-Elow usually begins in the late afternoon with men purchasing food for the *iftar*, the first meal after sunset. In the past, the male members of each clan in the village convened at their respective guest houses (*mandara*) to eat the *iftar* meal, for which each family in the clan sent a dish of food. This practice has recently become less frequent, however; most men now eat the *iftar* meal at their own homes, although guests may be invited for the occasion. In the evening, a festive air fills the narrow streets of the village as men crowd into the mosque for the *isha*, the fifth prayer of the day, and *il-tarawih*, a special prayer for Ramadan. Some male members of each clan will usually meet for the reading of the Koran and *il-tarawih* at their guest house, where a *mujid* (one who recites from the Koran) may read aloud until 2 or 3 A.M., when the *muezzin* announces on the radio or from the minarets that it is time to begin *sahur*, the meal eaten immediately before resumption of the fast at dawn. This meal generally consists of leftovers from the *iftar* feast. In addition, the *musahir* (village crier) roams the streets, rapping on doors with a stick and beating a drum to rouse the sleepy, and crying out in a loud voice, "Awake, sleepers! It is time for *sahur* and prayers!" The *musahir* often waits beneath the windows of particularly heavy sleepers until they acknowledge his call, usually with the sleepy reply, "Thank you, brother. May God compensate you with his grace and benevolence." At the end of Ramadan the *musahir* is usually given a few piasters by many of the villagers as a compensation for his services.

While all Muslims over the age of seventeen are expected to observe Ramadan, in many households of Kafr el-Elow even youngsters between the ages of ten and sixteen are encouraged to fast, although they are readily excused whenever they feel unable to continue the practice. However, I was told by several young informants that while elderly villagers generally abide by the Islamic fasting rules, many young adults do not. Some pretend to be fasting in public and in the company of their elders, but when alone, they smoke, drink, and eat as they please. Such "pretenders" usually get up with the rest of the family to eat *sahur*, but do not rejoin the family until after sunset for the *iftar* meal. Answers to a structured questionnaire administered to a group of young people between the ages of seventeen and twenty-five substantiated the informants' remarks, revealing that about 54 percent of the respondents did not fast regularly during the month of Ramadan. This finding was not unexpected, because the same situation exists in many urban areas of the Arab Middle East with which I am familiar.

The single most important religious event during the sacred month of Ramadan is the observance of *Laylat il-Qader*—the "Night of Power"—commemorating God's first revelation to the prophet Muhammad. While the event is celebrated on the twenty-seventh of the month, the original date has never been accurately determined. Devout Muslims believe that this is the time when the gates of heaven open and the favor of Allah descends upon them, because, according to Muhammad, of all the acts of worship in Islam, the sacrifice of Ramadan is the one which God alone sees and God alone rewards. Two or three days later occurs the official closing of the month of Ramadan with the appearance of the new moon for the month of Shawwal.

Aside from the religious significance of Ramadan, business activity increases tremendously during this period. Most of the people save all year in order that they may spend freely during Ramadan. Due to increased consumer demand, all prices rise during this period, but the price of meat, in particular, reflects the inflationary tendency. While the government ordinarily permits the sale of meat only four days each week in order to relieve the pressure on the meat supply, during the month of Ramadan butchers are allowed to sell meat daily. The fact that people greet one another during this month with the expression *Ramadan Kareem* (Ramadan is generous) and respond with *Wa Rabena Akram* (And God is more generous) reflects the spirit of generosity and hospitality that prevails in the village during the month of Ramadan.

### Az-Zakat—ALMSGIVING

Almsgiving, the fourth pillar of the Islamic religion, is explained by the Koran as follows:

If they ask you what they should give in alms, say "What can you spare?" Thus Allah makes plain to you his revelations, so that you may reflect upon this world and the hereafter. He that gives his wealth for the cause of Allah is like a grain of corn which brings forth seven ears, each bearing a hundred grains. Allah gives abundance to whom he wills; he is munificent and all-knowing. Those that give their wealth for the cause of Allah and do not follow their almsgiving with taunts and insults shall be rewarded by their lord; they shall have nothing to fear or to regret. A kind word with forgiveness is better than charity followed by insult. Allah is self-sufficient and indulgent. Believers, do not mar your almsgiving with taunts and mischief, making like those who spend their wealth for the sake of ostentation and believe neither in Allah nor in the Last Day. Such men are like a rock covered with earth: a shower falls upon it and leaves it hard and bare. They shall gain nothing from their works. Allah does not guide the unbelievers. But those that give away their wealth from a desire to please Allah and to reassure their own souls are like a garden on a hill-side: if a shower falls upon it, it yields up twice its normal crop; and if no rain falls upon it, it is watered by the dew. Allah takes cognizance of your actions. (Koran, 2:219, 261–265)

It is apparent from the above quotation that Islam expects those who are financially capable to give alms (*zakat*) to the poor. Almsgivers may make their contributions to the mosque in their community or to the *Waqf Ministry* (Ministry of Religious Affairs), the official government agency which distributes the funds for charitable purposes throughout Egypt wherever they are needed most.

Informants related that the villagers of Kafr el-Elow fulfill the almsgiving requirement of Islam in a variety of ways, sometimes doing this as a memorial to dead relatives and friends, and not always in the form of monetary donations. Those who kill sheep during religious holidays often sell the skins to a man who comes through the village periodically in order to collect sheep skins, giving the money derived in this manner to the Ministry of Religious Affairs for services to the needy. Others distribute meat to the poor during *Eid-il-Adha*, the sacrificial feast of Islam. Giving food and bread to beggars is still another form of almsgiving in Kafr el-Elow. Besides requiring donations for the poor, Islam's almsgiving obligation also enjoins Muslims to be hospitable and generous to all their guests and neighbors, irrespective of their economic condition.

### Al-Hajj—PILGRIMAGE TO MECCA

Pilgrimage to Mecca, the fifth and final pillar of Islam, is explained in the Koran as follows:

Fulfill the pilgrimage and the visitation unto God; but if you are prevented, then make such offering as may be feasible. And shave not your heads till the offering reaches its place of sacrifice. If any of you is sick or injured in his head, redemption will come by fasting, by free-will offering, or by ritual sacrifice. When you are secure, whosoever enjoys the visitation until the pilgrimage, let his offering be such as may be feasible; or if he finds none, then a fast of three days in the pilgrimage, and of seven when you return; that is, ten completely; that is for him whose family are not present at the Holy Mosque. And fear God, and know that God is terrible in retribution. The pilgrimage is in months well-known; whosoever undertakes the duty of pilgrimage in them shall not go into his womenfolk nor indulge in ungodliness and dissipating. Whatever good you do, God knows it. And take provision; but the best provision is God-fearing. So fear you Me, men possessed of minds! It is not fault in you that you should seek bounty from your Lord; but when you press on from Arafat, then remember God at the Holy Waymark, and remember Him as He has guided you, though formerly you were gone astray. (Koran, 2:92–94)

The prescribed direction (*qibla*) for Muslims to assume in reciting their daily prayers is facing Mecca, and pilgrimage to Mecca, the holiest city in the Islamic world, is one of the most exciting events in the lifetime of any Muslim. Devout Muslims pray ardently that God will enable them to make the trip before they die, and each year, during the month of *Thul-Hijah*, thousands of Muslims from all corners of the earth have this wish fulfilled. While devout Muslims regard pilgrimage to Mecca as a duty to God, they believe it is a sin for one to strain his financial resources to take the trip merely for the social esteem accorded him in his community upon returning from Mecca. Those who have completed the journey are referred to or addressed as *hajji* (males) or *hajja* (females), and it is believed that those who die on the way have been admitted directly to heaven (*firdaus*) by Allah. The latter are considered especially fortunate, because they are thought to have been selected by Allah for this privilege.

While this study was in progress (1964–1966), pilgrimage to Mecca by Egyptians was controlled by the Egyptian government, because the shortage of hard currency necessitated limitation on the number of persons leaving the country. Each year, following a certain deadline for application, the government indiscriminately drew the names of a specific number of persons to fill the quota for the trip to Mecca. During my first year in Kafr el-Elow, none of the village applicants' names were drawn by the government to make the pilgrimage to Mecca, but during my second year, two people from the village were selected. A week before they departed for Mecca, both men, following village tradition, entertained many relatives and friends at their respective guest houses and discussed their forthcoming trip. The guests, in turn, wished them a safe journey, requested a remembrance in their prayers at Mecca, and gave them farewell gifts (*nkout*). The usual gift on such an occasion is money, varying in amount from one-half Egyptian pound to five Egyptian pounds, to help defray the traveler's expenses and to serve as an incentive for him to buy the donor a souvenir in Mecca.

On the departure day itself, the pilgrims dressed in white clothing and were led in a procession through Kafr el-Elow so that their relatives and friends could bid them farewell. Then both men were taken by their relatives in taxis to Port Said where they embarked by ship for Mecca. The writer was told by some informants in the village that in the past a few of the villagers had traveled by plane to Mecca, but this mode of transportation is more expensive than is traveling by ship.

A few days before the pilgrims returned home to Kafr el-Elow, their families whitewashed their homes in preparation for inscribing the doors and walls with verses from the Koran commemorating the pilgrims' journey to Mecca. In addition, a ship was painted on the outside wall of each house to signify the mode of transportation. Informants told me that pilgrims who travel by plane to Mecca, and on whose homes a plane is painted, enjoy higher social status or prestige among the villagers than do those who travel by ship. On the day of their return from Mecca, the pilgrims were met at Port Said by their relatives, who had set up a large tent in Kafr el-Elow where for about a week, the travelers received kin and friends who came to congratulate them on their achievement. Arriving at the pilgrims' home, the kin and friends kissed the travelers' cheeks and said, *hajj mabrouk* (a blessed pilgrimage); the travelers replied, *oukbal endak* (may the Almighty provide you also to make the trip). Some of the pilgrims' close relatives sent baskets filled with sugar, rice and tea and other beverages to their homes, understanding that it is a considerable strain on any family's financial resources to entertain guests for a week. The guests were also served some of the meat from a sheep which the pilgrims' families had slaughtered in gratitude for their safe return from Mecca (*karamat*). A portion of the meat was also given to the poor of the village.

Throughout the pilgrims' welcome-home week, female and male relatives gathered separately to perform certain rituals, such as singing and dancing, to celebrate their return from Mecca. On the seventh day following their return, the pilgrims distributed gifts which they had brought from Mecca—beads, silver rings and bracelets, shawls, tablecloths, wall tapestries, pieces of material for clothing, incense and herbs—many of which had been manufactured in Japan or Hong Kong. Recipients of these gifts—members of the immediate families, relatives, and friends who had given them money on their departure—were both materially and spiritually satisfied by the mere facts that the items were purchased in Mecca and that the pilgrims had remembered them.

## Islam's Impact on the Villagers

Islam is a system of beliefs and practices based on the Koran, and emphasizes submission (*aslama*) to God's Will: "Allah misleads whom He wills." The villagers contended throughout a great variety of situations that "nothing happens except by God's Will (*La-yassebukum il-la-wa-Makataba Allah lakum*). When a "good" (religious) man's crops failed or livestock died, it was interpreted as God testing the faith of a man He loves, whereas if the same tragedy befell an irreligious man's property, it was interpreted as God's punishment for some sin(s) the individual had committed. Even a simple question, such as whether he were going out to work in his fields or were going to take a trip to Helwan on a certain day, would typically elicit the response: "Whatever God wills" (*In sha Allah*).

This dependence on God's will is expressed primarily by older villagers. On one of my regular visits to the tailor shop, I was asked by the tailor's nineteen-year-old son for a ride the following week to Cairo, for he wished to attend the celebration there commemorating Muhammad's birthday. Although his father objected strenuously, telling his son that he needed his help at the shop, the son insisted on going to Cairo. Finally, his father suggested that his son should say, "I wish to go to Cairo next week, if God wills it." However, the son insisted that he was going to Cairo regardless of circumstances, and his father shook his head and told me: "These days, young people have no faith in God. My son insists on going to Cairo even against God's Will, not realizing that God could strike him dead at this moment if He wished." When I was about to leave the shop, the young man said, with a smile on his face: "Don't forget to pass by next week and pick me up."

Islam makes no distinction between the sacred and the profane in life, covering by divine ordinance every moment of each day, and every situation which could possibly arise from the time of birth to that of death. In other words, Islam comprehends life in its totality, and as long as the Muslim conforms to the particular way of life prescribed by the prophet, "he is fortified by the assurance of his righteousness" (Grunebaum 1953:108).

> Why should we not believe in God and the truth that has come to us, and be eager that our Lord should admit us with the righteous people? And God will reward them for what they say with gardens underneath where rivers flow, therein dwelling forever; that is the recompense of the good-doers. But those who disbelieve . . . are the inhabitants of Hell. (Koran, 5:87–88)

Two stories dramatically illustrate the power of reward and punishment over the lives of most villagers in Kafr el-Elow. One story concerns a mother-in-law who attempted to poison her son's wife after serious conflict developed between her and the girl over the newlywed couple's marital difficulties. Instead of the girl's eating the poisoned food which her mother-in-law had prepared and set aside for her, the young husband came home unusually early from work that day, ate the poisoned food, and died instantly. The second story concerns a man who perjured himself by swearing falsely on the Koran that he had already repaid a loan to one of his creditors when the latter sent a village leader to his home as a mediator in order to collect the money which had been borrowed. Later that same day, one of the perjurer's water buffaloes was killed by a truck. According to informants, the moral that the villagers drew from both incidents was that Allah is aware of everything that happens and is sometimes swift in punishing evildoers.

On the other hand, informants told me that the villagers also believe that Allah is merciful and compassionate, frequently suspending His punishment and granting an evildoer a long life so that he has a chance to change his ways and make amends for past moral violations. Barclay, in his study of the Sudanese village, Buurri al Lamaab, seems to suggest a similar notion by his statement that "particularly in a religion which emphasizes a final day of judgement and doctrines of heaven and hell, as Islam does, a man might become more concerned about religious matters as he approaches old age and death" (Barclay 1964:143).

Three practices condemned by Islam are eating pork, drinking alcoholic beverages, and gambling. However, the first of these prohibitions is the only one that is rigidly observed in Kafr el-Elow, for the simple reason that pork cannot be purchased in, or anywhere near, the village. Since the early 1960s, beer has been sold by two grocers in Kafr el-Elow, as well as by the village coffee shop. Most of the villagers drinking beer are young factory workers who rationalize the practice by saying that since beer is made from barley, it must be a healthful beverage. Nevertheless, they usually drink it secretly behind a screen in the grocery store or at private hashish-smoking parties. Gambling, the third prohibited practice, which is likewise forbidden by Egyptian civil law, is also a popular activity at young villagers' beer-drinking and hashish-smoking parties. It usually consists of playing cards for money. Several years ago, the authorities closed a coffee shop in Kafr el-Elow while gambling and hashish-smoking were in progress.

# Universal Islamic Practices

## HOLIDAYS AND FESTIVITIES

Three major festivals are celebrated by all Muslims, including the villagers of Kafr el-Elow: *eid il-Fitr* or *il-eid-il saghir* (the little feast); *eid-il-adha* or *il-eid-il-kabir* (the big feast); and *mawlid an-nabawi* (the birthday of the Prophet).

*Eid il-Fitr* (the little feast), comes at the end of the fasting month of Ramadan. Since this, like most Egyptian festivals, is a family affair, the absence of the deceased members of each family unit is felt acutely. In consequence, the festivals begin with religious rituals. On the first day of the festival, men go to the mosque very early to offer morning prayers (*salat es-subh*). In the meantime, the women go to the cemetery, taking along cookies (*fatir*) and fruits (*kahik*) to distribute to the beggars and children who tend to congregate there early in the morning. After morning prayer service at the mosque, the males join the women at the cemetery, although they stand some distance apart, and the women bring to a sudden halt the wailing and crying in which they have been engaged prior to the men's arrival.

During the *eid il-Fitr* festival, a *mukre* (one who recites from the Koran) is frequently called to the cemetery to recite the *Fatiha* over the tombs of the villagers' relatives, in return for which he receives bread, cookies, fruits, and occasionally, money. Before the rituals at the cemetery come to an end, the men exchange the holiday greeting: *kul am wa inta tayib* (hope to see you healthy and happy at all times). Then they proceed to their respective clan guest houses where holiday greetings are exchanged again, and their children—both boys and girls—kiss the hands of the elderly, hoping to be given some money which they can spend on candy or on amusement rides that are provided by some of the local shopkeepers as well as by itinerant amusement companies which come to the village during the festival periods. Everyone is dressed in his or her best clothing, especially the children whose garments are brightly colored, in keeping with the joyousness of the occasion. Members of different clans also exchange visits on *eid il-Fitr*, going to each other's guest houses to extend their holiday greetings. Tea or soft drinks are usually served at such times. While the *eid il-Fitr* festival lasts three days and is a civil as well as a religious holiday period, the first day is most important because of the religious activities on this day.

*Eid-il-adha* (the big feast), resembles the first holiday in several ways: (1) both last three days, the first of which is the most significant; (2) both open with congregational prayers by the men at the village mosque, after which many villagers visit the cemetery to read the *Fatiha* in memory of deceased relatives and friends; and, (3) some adults, especially young men of the younger generation, attend movies in Helwan or Cairo during the three days of both festivals, while parents frequently visit their married daughters, especially those who have wed outside the clan, and give them gifts of money, usually between one-half pound and two pounds. In contrast, however, since *eid-il-adha* is the festival of sacrifices, those who are financially capable are expected to buy a sheep and to slaughter it after morning prayer on the first day. In the village of Kafr el-Elow, butchers do most of the slaughtering for those who buy animals for the occasion. Some of the villagers do kill their own animals, and were frequently seen dipping their hands in the blood of the animal after slaying it preparatory to making imprints on the outside doors of their homes as a sign that they have sacrificed a sheep during the festival period. Considerable prestige is derived from this ritual.

The sheep-slaying ritual supposedly commemorates the occasion when God was so pleased by the prophet Abraham's willingness to obey the Divine Command to sacrifice his son, Ishmael, that He ordered the prophet to slaughter a lamb instead. Islamic tradition prescribes that two-thirds of the slaughtered animal shall be distributed among the poor and that the remaining one-third shall be consumed by members of the household offering the sacrifice. It is not generally acceptable for a person to send meat to a poor relative because it might hurt the relative's pride, but some of the villagers do so in spite of this possibility. However, most of the villagers distribute the meat to transient agricultural workers, to beggars, and to poor, recently-arrived residents of the village. The portion of the meat to be consumed by the family is cooked, after which it is generally placed on top of a thin bread (*battawi*), which has been soaked with the meat juice, and is served in the guest house on a brass dish (*anker*) to the male members of the clan following their return from the cemetery on the first day of the festival. Tea is usually served after the meal, and at this time members of the clan exchange holiday greetings.

As is true preceding the *eid il-Fitr* festival, an outsider who visits Kafr el-Elow one or two days before the *eid-il-adha* festival observes the villagers spending more money than usual on sweets, vegetables, meat, and other food items to be consumed during the holiday festivities. The tailor shop in the village stays open all night on the day preceding the festivals in order to finish customers' orders, and both the barber and pressing shops are much more crowded than usual. A few villagers—those who are well-off financially and who have a recently-deceased relative—rent loud speaker equipment to set up in front of their homes on the night when they hire a *mukre* to recite the Koran in memory of their departed ones.

*Mawlid an-Nabawi*, the third major religious festival celebrated in the village of Kafr el-Elow and throughout Egypt, begins on the eve of the eleventh day of the month of Rabi al-Awal (third month in the Islamic lunar calendar) and commemorates the birth of the prophet Muhammad. However, the villagers of Kafr el-Elow start celebrating this festival four days before the twelfth of Rabi al-Awal, which is the prophet's actual birth date. Those financially able usually decorate their homes and build big tents on the open spaces adjacent to their homes where male guests and relatives will eat their holiday meals and participate in the prescribed religious rituals. Some celebrate the occasion in order to fulfill a vow (*nadar*) which they have made to God. On any of the evenings prior to the festival day itself, recitations from the Koran about the life of Muhammad as well as chants of the people praising Allah, can be heard over microphones throughout the village.

In addition to the celebration of *mawlid an-nabawi* by individuals in the village, the various religious brotherhoods (*il-touruq-is-soufiya*) sponsor festivities on two evenings prior to Muhammad's birthday. Members of each brotherhood (*tariqa*) meet. On these occasions, either at the home of their director or in a tent erected specifically for their purposes. On their first evening of celebration, besides recitations from the Koran and praises to the prophet, the members of each brotherhood march forward and backward in two parallel lines chanting the following verses: *Zikr Allah* (The name of God, the compassionate and merciful), *al hayy al gayyum* (Who is living and present everywhere), *al tawheed lil-lah* (God, he is the one). During their second evening of celebration, on the day preceding Muhammad's birthday, all the religious brotherhoods in Kafr el-Elow join the villagers in a procession led by flagbearers and a band from a neighboring village, chanting praises to the prophet of Islam as they march.

Most families in the village of Kafr el-Elow celebrate Muhammad's birthday, a legal holiday throughout Egypt, by eating a big meal in their respective homes. A few commemorate the feast by going to Cairo's Essit Zainab Mosque, one of the country's most famous mosques which is located in the old section of the city, and renting a room or a spot in one of the big tents erected around the mosque for two or three days. Still others go to nearby Helwan to celebrate the prophet's birthday. During the festivities connected with Muhammad's birthday, merchants come with their wagons to the village of Kafr el-Elow in order to sell cotton candy and *arusa*, a brightly-colored candy doll which is an Egyptian symbol for Muhammad's birthday.

### CIRCUMCISION AND CLITORIDECTOMY (*il-tahuur*)

Although circumcision is not prescribed by the Koran, it has become a universal practice for the male offspring of orthodox Muslims. In Kafr el-Elow, as in other Egyptian peasant communities, many female children as well must undergo a similar ritual called clitoridectomy, but whereas circumcision is marked by joyous celebration, clitoridectomy is a quiet and secret affair.

Traditionally, the boy to be circumcised, who is usually between the ages of four and seven and who is called *arees* (groom), is led in a small procession to the front of his home where invited guests and relatives clap to the beat of drums and utter cries of joy (*zagareet*). Following the procession, the boy is seated on a chair and prepared for circumcision by the traditional village barber, who then performs the operation with a razor blade and scissors while the boy's female relatives observe the ritual, clapping and shouting for joy. Recently, the barber began sterilizing his instruments with alcohol, after discovering that an increasing number of parents were taking their sons to clinics for circumcision, as the result of a growing awareness that any incision will heal faster if the surgery is performed by a doctor under sterile conditions. An additional impetus is the fact that public clinics charge no fee for circumcision.

While this new trend has led to a gradual decline in ritual elaboration by the families of circumcised boys, guests and relatives are still invited to the home for a meal to celebrate the event, at which time they are usually expected to give the boy a gift of money (*nkout*) varying in amount from one-half pound to two pounds. All or part of this money is frequently used to pay for the food which has been prepared for the guests and to compensate the traditional village barber, whose fee for performing circumcisions varies from one-half pound to one pound, depending upon the financial capacity of the family. The two modern barbers in Kafr el-Elow told me that they will not perform circumcisions because they are of the opinion that this is more properly the role of a physician operating in a clinic setting.

Circumcisions are also performed in Kafr el-Elow by an itinerant who travels from one village to another carrying his instruments in a bag inscribed with the Arabic word *muttahir* "circumcisor." Upon arriving in a village, the muttahir calls out, *muttahir awlad, muttahir awlad* (a professional circumcisor for boys). Despite the fact that the muttahir's fee is less than that of the traditional barber, very few villagers in Kafr el-Elow, with the exception of newcomers and those who are so poor that they cannot afford any celebration of the circumcision ritual, utilize his services.

Although female clitoridectomy is prohibited by law in Egypt, it is still practiced in rural areas of the country. In the village of Kafr el-Elow, some females undergo clitoridectomy at puberty by a *ghagarieh* (gypsy) who travels from village to village "circumcising" young girls and tatooing women. Whereas in the past the *ghagarieh's* fee was only ten piasters plus a bar of soap and some corn, it is now twenty-five to fifty piasters, depending on the income of the girl's family. The girl to be "circumcised" usually sits on her grandmother's or her mother's lap facing the *ghagarieh*, while a female relative holds her legs apart. The *ghagarieh* then cuts the girl's clitoris and the lips of her vulva with a razor blade. After the operation, the wound may be rubbed with oven ashes to minimize bleeding. Other folk remedies used to treat the cuts are the juice of an onion or the fried and ground leaves of the sant tree (*aras*). In the past, "circumcised" girls would also sit in the canal (*tura*) during the night, in accordance with the belief that the silt from the Nile waters would help to heal their incisions. Today, however, girls usually treat the sore area in the privacy of their homes, and an increasing number are using antibiotic and sulfa drugs to prevent infection from setting in. Most female clitoridectomies take place during the fall and winter months, because it is believed that the cooler weather facilitates blood coagulation and the healing of wounds.

As I indicated at the beginning of this section, female clitoridectomies are not publicly celebrated, and about the only recognition of the girls' ordeal is the preparation of several pigeons and chickens so that they can eat heartily for at least a week and quickly replace the blood which they have lost. The usual explanations given by the villagers of Kafr el-Elow for this practice were that it is traditional (*halal*) and that it reduces the female's sexual desire so that she will not run after boys as an adolescent or be unfaithful to her husband as a married woman. Another reason advanced by some village informants was that clitoridectomy makes a female's vaginal opening smaller, thereby enhancing her future husband's sexual enjoyment. However, this practice has decreased lately.

## DEATH RITES

In the village of Kafr el-Elow, death is not only regarded as a rite of passage, but also as an occasion that reflects the solidarity of the deceased person's clan and gives the villagers an opportunity to express their sympathy. In the past, screamed and wailed so loudly that in a short time the news spread throughout the entire village. In recent years, as a result of the village's expansion, news of a death whenever a death occurred in Kafr el-Elow, the deceased person's female relatives is circulated by a man who, for a fee of about ten piasters, goes around the village beating a drum and shouting the name of the deceased person. Subsequently, relatives and neighbors come to the dead person's home, where the women congregate, wailing, shrieking, and repeating the name of the deceased over and over again. As soon as all the relatives have assembled, the corpse is placed on a bench and washed with soap and water by the village tailor (if the deceased is a male), who performs the task free of charge. The body of a dead woman is washed by a female. The practice of washing corpses is based on the Islamic belief that the dead should be made clean and pure before meeting Allah.

After the *mughassil* (washer of the dead) has washed the corpse, he sprinkles it with perfume or rose water, blesses it with holy water from the *Zam-zam* well in Mecca, and places pieces of cotton in the ears and nose. Finally, he wraps the corpse in white cotton material and places it in a bier which is covered with a piece of green material decorated with verses from the Koran. While the *mughassil* prepares the corpse, a *mukre* recites from the Koran, the women continue their wailing and shrieking, and the male relatives and neighbors sit in an adjacent room or stand outside the house waiting for the funeral. Some of the deceased person's relatives and friends contribute their services to the death rites by sewing the shroud (the white cloth in which the corpse is wrapped), by carrying the bier, or by digging the grave. According to Islamic belief, those who render such services, referred to as *halal* or *ajr*, will be rewarded by Allah.

In accord with Islamic tradition and the Arabic proverb (*dafin il mayyit halal*) the dead are buried as soon as possible. Persons who die before noon are usually buried on the same day, and those who die in the afternoon are usually buried the following morning. Four men generally carry the bier from the deceased person's home, and the female relatives continue their wailing and crying. The women usually follow the funeral procession for a few yards, but are then ordered by the men to return to the house. While the funeral procession makes its way to the cemetery (*il-jabbana* or *garafa*), which is located at the extreme east side of the village, the men recite the *Fatiha* and other verses from the Koran in loud voices, and groups of four take turns carrying the bier.

Two types of graves may be observed at the cemetery. One type, built to accommodate extended families, consists of a small room which is divided into two sections: one for males and one for females. This room, which is usually constructed of stone, has a cement roof and is built underground, with only two or three feet appearing above the ground level. Informants told me that there are fewer than six such graves in Kafr el-Elow, all built within the past ten years. The second type, the conventional single grave, is much more prevalent, because it is less expensive to construct. It generally requires the efforts of two men to place the corpse in a niche in the side of the grave so that it lies on its right side facing Mecca (*qibla*). Then long stones are placed on top of the grave to keep out the sand, and in many cases, wet dirt is used to seal the holes between the stones. After this is done, those present recite the *Fatiha* and the *shaik* or the *mukre* recites other verses to the dead person: "O servant of God, when you are asked by the two angels who is your God, say 'Allah is my God and the prophet Muhammad is his messenger.' And when you are asked about your religion, say, 'Islam is your faith and the Koran is your guide.'"

Immediately following the burial service, the male relatives of the deceased stand in a line at the cemetery to accept condolences from friends and neighbors, some of whom express their sympathy by hugging and kissing, while others simply shake hands and say, "May God have mercy on the departed one's soul so that he will be placed in heaven, and may God prolong your life." Then the men return to their respective homes, while the immediate family of the deceased prepares to accept condolences during a period of from three days to a week at its guest house or in a big tent set up especially for this purpose. The head and the elderly members of the deceased person's clan, as well as the *shaik* of the village mosque, stay in the guest house or tent almost constantly during the *azaa* (mourning period) in order to receive guests. The hosts greet guests with a handshake and the greeting, *shakara-Allah sayukum* (May God reward you for your effort), to which the guests reply, *kghafara Allah thanbakoum* (May God also forgive you your sins). Then the guests are seated, those with high status being given the most comfortable places, even if this necessitates the removal of an occupant. I experienced this situation in Kafr el-Elow when my research assistant and I went to the home of a deceased person to extend condolences to his family. As we entered the house, two elderly men arose and insisted that we take their places on the sofa, an extraordinary gesture of hospitality considering that they were not even members of the deceased person's clan. Although the floor of the guest house is covered with carpets, chairs are available to seat those who wear western-style suits.

A microphone is usually set up in front of the house or tent so that the *mukre*'s recitations from the Koran, for which he is paid one Egyptian pound, may be heard throughout the village. During the visitation, cigarettes and coffee are offered to the guests, the coffee (*kahwa sada*) served in small cups with no sugar or cream. On such an occasion, people tend to talk a great deal about life and death and about the power of Allah. Upon leaving the mourning rituals, guests are accompanied to the door by one or two members of the deceased person's family, who once again shake their hands and thank them for coming.

On the Thursday morning of the week following a burial, the deceased person's female relatives usually visit the grave to wail and cry; then they distribute cookies (*fatir*) to all present. Relatives of the deceased who are financially well-off celebrate the end of the mourning period by killing a sheep or a goat and by inviting all available villagers to their homes for a big meal. This last ritual in behalf of the deceased is referred to as *karama*.

Several important changes in the traditional mourning rituals have taken place during the past fifteen years in Kafr el-Elow. Whereas the mourning period formerly lasted forty days, now it never continues longer than one week, because most people have less free time to devote to such rituals and because of the tremendous increase in the cost of the food served to the guests. Throughout the former forty-day mourning period, male members of the deceased person's immediate family refrained from shaving, the female members wore dark clothes and no jewelry, refrained from combing their hair, and did not bake bread or cook, relying upon relatives and friends to supply them with food. Today, the only one of these customs that has been preserved is the wearing of dark clothing by the deceased person's female kin. Finally, whereas the entire clan of a deceased person traditionally sat around his grave throughout the night of the first holiday after his death, they now visit his grave on the morning of the holiday, and the male relatives assemble during the evening of the same day at the guest house to express and receive condolences.

## Practices Associated with Islam in Kafr el-Elow

### THE EVIL EYE (*ain il-hasud*)

In the village of Kafr el-Elow, as in Egypt generally, there is a belief in the destructive power of the "evil eye" (*ain il-hasud* or *el ain il wihshah*), which is referred to in both the Koran and Islamic tradition (Hadith).

> In the name of God, the Merciful, the Compassionate, say: "I take refuge with the lord of the Daybreak from the evil of what he has created, from the evil of darkness when it gathers, from the evil of the women who blow on knots, from the evil of an envier when he arrives." (Koran, 113:1–5)

According to Muslim belief, individuals possessed by the evil eye (comparable to the devil) have no control over its power and, indeed, may not even be conscious of why they perform certain evil deeds or are victims of various misfortunes. Consequently, in order to protect their children and livestock, the villagers of Kafr el-Elow avoid talking about them, especially to strangers, because it is believed that another's envy can result in the possession of the person or thing envied by the evil eye. I frequently encountered reluctance on the part of the villagers to answer questions regarding the number of their children, especially the number of male offspring, and their place of employment. If, however, I prefaced my questioning with the statement: *Allah ye zeed wa ye barik* (May God increase and bless your house), the villagers were more spontaneous and frank in providing me with the information requested, and reciprocated by saying, *rabina yezeedak min neamouh* (May the Almighty increase His blessing upon you).

Another phenomenon observed in Kafr el-Elow which demonstrates the villagers' fear of the evil eye is the midwives' practice of concealing the sex of the babies they deliver from everyone but those in attendance, to whom they reveal the news by using certain symbols. For example, whenever a female baby is born, the midwife simply covers her as a protection against the evil eye and leaves; if the baby is a boy, the midwife not only covers him, but also tells the parents verbally that they have a girl in an effort to deceive the evil spirits, hangs a golden palm over his head, and may pierce one of his ears and insert an earring: all for the purpose of protecting him against the evil eye. Later, when relatives, and occasionally neighbors, are shown the baby, they are expected to say, *ma sha Allah* (the power of God is so great), and then recite a prayer. According to Muslim belief, if such a procedure is followed, the evil eye will be powerless to do harm to the infant.

Even after their children are several years old, mothers employ various devices to reduce their susceptibility to the evil eye's influence. It is hoped on the one hand, that by dressing a child in brightly-colored clothes the evil eye will be attracted to the clothes rather than to the child itself; on the other hand, a child may be dressed in old clothes in order to repel the evil eye. If, in spite of all the mother's precautions, a child becomes ill and the sickness is attributed to the evil eye, the child's mother or grandmother, or perhaps a female ritualist in the village, will burn incense, wrapping the ashes in a piece of cloth along with a piaster; the package will then be dropped on a street where many people pass, the woman hoping that whoever picks it up will contract the child's illness, thereby relieving the child and causing him to recover. I observed a similar ritual employed for the same purpose in Jordan, whereby the sick child's grandmother, after burning charcoal or wood in a metal tray, then throwing salt into the flames producing a crackling sound, rotated the tray over the child's head or walked around the baby as it lay in its crib or in its mother's lap. In other cases, incense is simply burned near the sick child with the intention of chasing away the evil spirit and inviting the angels to take its place.

In Kafr el-Elow and throughout the Arab Middle East, one also observes many adults following a custom similar to a widespread American practice; namely, that of placing a St. Christopher medal, a rosary, or a plastic statue of Christ, the Virgin Mary, or a saint somewhere near the dashboards of their cars for protection against accidents. Muslims hang a piece of palm with an eye-shaped hole cut in the center or a blue bead from the mirrors of their cars. Many villagers also place a charm on the step or over the door of the main entrance to their homes to protect themselves from the evil eye. They purchase these charms in jewelry stores or in shops that sell folk medicine supplies.

## THE CULT OF CHARMS

According to Islamic tradition (*Hadith*), the prophet Muhammad sanctioned the use of charms only (*hejab*) for protection against the evil eye. In Kafr el-Elow, however, charms are also used, especially by women, as protective devices against sickness, accidents, and ill fate in general. The *hejab* is also used as a means of treatment for those who are already sick, both physically and emotionally.

There is one charm practitioner whose popularity extends beyond Kafr el-Elow, who inherited the role from his father upon the latter's death. His father left him a book containing prescriptions for the treatment of various physical and mental diseases, the title and publisher of which he refused to reveal even to the writer, lest the information fall into the hands of persons who might use it for evil-doing. The charm practitioner's main profession is tailoring, but when a client comes to his shop seeking help, he usually locks the door so that nobody will disturb him. The majority of his clients are women seeking improvement in their marital relations, termination of their husbands' impotence or adulterous behavior, the prevention of a male relative's marriage outside of his clan or village, or the breaking of such a union in the hope that their daughters' marriage opportunities will thereby improve. It is interesting to note that while the practitioner agrees to oppose exogamous marriages, he considers it a sin to interfere with endogamous marriages, which are the preferred type in the village. Another major reason why female villagers seek the practitioner's aid is to assure long life for their newborn babies, since the mortality rate for infants in Kafr el-Elow under one year of age is nearly 25 percent.

The practitioner cited to me two cases that he had cured, although he maintained that it had been possible only because God had so willed. One was that of an impotent man whom he had cured by giving two charms, one to pin to his undershirt and the other to put under his pillow. After following the practitioner's prescription for several nights, the man was able to perform the sex act without difficulty. A patient with a nagging backache was the second case cited by the practitioner. After doctors in Helwan and Cairo were unable to relieve his condition, the patient visited the charm practitioner in Kafr el-Elow, where he first undressed and then lay down on a mat while the practitioner wrote and drew signs with a red ballpoint pen over the patient's entire body, beginning with the spots that hurt most. Later the charm practitioner went to the patient's home and bathed him in warm water while burning incense and reciting the *Fatiha*. Since this treatment, for which the practitioner charged three Egyptian pounds, the patient has felt extremely well.

The practitioner's treatment appears to be largely psychotherapeutic, for by allowing his patients to set their own fees, which are not payable unless or until cures are effected, the practitioner induces his clients to have confidence in his curative powers. The charms themselves are simply triangular or rectangular pieces of paper inscribed with various symbols and Arabic phrases and covered with triangular-shaped cloth, like those pictured below.

 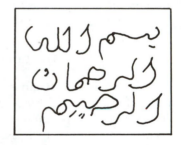

The ZAR Cult

*Figure 14. The Zar Cult*

The *zar* cult, the central feature of which is the practice of casting out demons, is believed to have been introduced to Egypt sometime during the late eighteenth or early nineteenth century by female Ethiopian slaves who entertained the harems of the rich Pashas, Beys, and other wealthy families (Behman 1953:11). With the passage of time and the increased population mobility, the cult diffused to the lower classes, which found it highly consistent with their existing beliefs in supernatural beings, magic, sacrifice, and the inferior status of women (most of the *zar* spirits' victims are women).

There are two kinds of *zar*: public and private. First, I will describe the public *zar* which is conducted every Friday at the Shrine of *Shaik* Mahfouz in Kafr el-Elow, except during the month of Ramadan. (Since, according to the interpretation of the Koran, evil spirits disappear during the month of Ramadan, there is no necessity for the *zar* at that time.) Those who come to the shrine for the relief of their symptoms arrive around noon, remove their shoes, pay a fee of two piasters, and then proceed to the room containing the *shaik's* tomb, which they occasionally touch to bless themselves as they walk around it reading from the Koran.

Next, they go to an adjoining room where the *zar* practitioner, who may be either a man or a woman, diagnoses their maladies and attempts, if this is their first *zar*, to identify the spirits which possess them. Since music is a prime instrument of the healing process, the actual *zar* rituals begin once the musicians—a flutist, drummer, and tambourinist—have assembled.

As the music prescribed by the practitioner for her patients progresses, the possessed women sway from side to side until their spirits respond to the beat (*dakka*), at which time some give the practitioner a tip varying from two to ten piasters. While the musicians are playing, they and the practitioner sing certain songs appropriate to the spirits possessing the women who are attending the *zar*. The following, for example, is a verse from the song to the spirit *il-sultan il-ahmar* (Red Sultan): "Red King of Kings, ye the King of ginnies, recall your spirits so that all of them will be present. . . . Oh you little bride holding a lighted candle in your hand, you are the bride of the Sultan, and your groom is like a lighted candle." If the patient is a victim of the spirit *il-nabi* (the Prophet), the appropriate song includes these words: "Oh beloved prophet, oh beloved prophet, oh beloved prophet, bless your spirit; she is your subject and your presence is always welcome."

As the musicians play their instruments and sing, the patients customarily beat their chests, breathe heavily, wail or shout for joy, and eventually, as the music becomes louder and louder, stand up and dance wildly until they go into a trance and faint from exhaustion. While dancing, each patient who is partici-

*Village shrine*

pating in her second or subsequent *zar* wears a gown (*jalabiya*) of the color previously prescribed by the practitioner as demanded by the particular spirit possessing her. The gown is worn to the *zar* under the black *jalabiya* which is the customary dress for village women and which is removed before the dance commences. All the patients—old and new—wear a facial veil during their respective dances to conceal the ugly expressions they will make after going into a trance, from which they are revived by the practitioner or an accompanying relative through body massaging and a drink of water. In addition to forcing the *zar* spirits to reveal themselves, the patients' ritualistic dancing has some very important secondary functions: the release of their pent-up energies, repressed sexual urges, and other emotions.

Once the patients' *zar* spirits have revealed themselves, the practitioner attempts to convert them from evil to protective spirits. This is achieved by imploring the spirits to reveal what rituals their victims must perform in order to eliminate or mitigate their torments. Certain *zar* spirits' demands are easily fulfilled, sometimes by having the patient's wear specific types of jewelry and silk clothing. A woman possessed by *sayed il-dair* (spirit of the monastery), for example, may be asked to wear priests' clothing, drink wine, and follow the Coptic fasts and festivals. The spirit *il-sultan il-ahmar* (Red Sultan) may demand that his victims wear a red cloak, present him with red candles, and sacrifice red roosters or chickens; the spirit *is-sudani* (the Sudanese) may require the wearing of a green *jalabiya* and the sacrificing of a goat; the spirit *il-habashi* (the Ethiopian) may request the sacrificing of both a male and female turkey; the spirit *il-nabi* (the prophet) may demand the wearing of a white *jalabiya* and the sacrificing of a lamb or a pair of pigeons. Other spirits' alleged demands, however, are not only less easy, but are also more expensive, to fulfill.

Since very few *zar* cult patients are discharged as permanently cured, most of them attend public *zar* frequently, sometimes over a period of several years. But the persistent attendance is also accounted for by the social and psychological aspects of the rituals; namely, the opportunity to make personal contacts and to vicariously participate in others' emotional experiences.

In addition to the public *zar*, private *zar* are conducted at any time by the village practitioner at the homes of the possessed. The home where a private *zar* is being conducted is usually brightly lighted by candles, filled with the odor of incense, and crowded with an assemblage of guests wearing brightly colored dresses who sit on pillows tastefully arranged on a carpeted floor. During a private *zar*, the practitioner and the musicians direct all the rituals to the possessed person sponsoring the ceremony, unless he or she is sharing the *zar* with a few possessed guests. In such cases, the guests also share the expenses, which may match or even exceed those of a wedding. Another factor differentiating a private from a public *zar* is that in the former, the sacrifices allegedly demanded by the possessing spirit are carried out by the practitioner at the home of the hostess and on the same day the rituals are performed; the latter, on the contrary, may be carried out several days or weeks later by the patients in their respective homes.

The following case histories of alleged possession by evil spirits—this possession having occurred in the most frequently sited locations: cemeteries and bathrooms—were provided me by the *zar* practitioner in Kafr el-Elow and illustrate both patient symptomatology and the treatment involved in a typical *zar* ceremony.

PATIENT NUMBER ONE    This is a woman in her forties who has been married twice. As a child she fainted of fright in a cemetery. Her mother used incense to help her recover from the experience and then took her to a male *zar* practitioner (*shaik*), who prescribed the sacrificing of a pair of pigeons and the blessing of the child with their blood. The mother was also advised to buy her daughter jewelry specifically designed to repel the evil spirits that were causing her headaches and her troubles with her brothers and sisters. The ornaments consisted of two silver rings engraved with the words, *Allah Akbar* (God is great), a fetish made from a brown stone to be pinned in her hair, and a necklace with a red stone to protect her heart. During her first marriage, the young woman's internal problems manifested themselves again. This time, she was in continuous conflict with her husband and she imagined that Negroes were trying to kill her. Upon consulting another *shaik,* she was told that she was possessed by the spirit *Abdel Salam El-Soudani* and that to satisfy him she had to sponsor or attend a *zar* ceremony, wear a white dress, sacrifice a sea pigeon and a red rooster, put their blood on her head, and not go out for a week. She felt so much better after participating in a *zar* as the *shaik* had recommended that she has not missed a single one since that time. During her first pregnancy she sacrificed several fowl, hoping to thereby prevent the evil spirits from killing her baby at birth. Now that the patient is older, however, she suffers from pains in her head and legs which, she contends, are punishment because she has not obeyed her spirit's directives. Now she is willing to do anything to please the spirit and to secure relief from her distress, because doctors are not able to cure her and only make her feel worse.

PATIENT NUMBER TWO    This is a woman in her thirties who, at the age of twelve, was hit by her brother in the privy of her home. As a result of the blow she felt nauseated, her face was swollen, her eyes stared, and she refused food. A *shaik* consulted by her mother attributed the child's condition to possession by a *rieh* (spirit of a bathroom) and recommended that the girl attend a *zar*. The mother refused to comply with his advice, however, and the girl's sickness grew worse daily. Often she felt that people were jumping on her when she was in the bathroom. Finally, the girl's grandmother took her to a *zar*, and for three consecutive weeks thereafter the girl visited Mari Guirguis and Amir Tadros Churches as the *zar* practitioner had ordered, running about kissing the crosses and statues each time. After completing the church visits, she regained her appetite and began to act normal. Now, whenever the patient feels nervous or aggressive, she attends a *zar* ceremony.

Zar practitioners usually claim, to justify sanction for their alleged ability to cure the possessed, that they have inherited the prerequisite powers and knowledge from relatives. Some maintain, however, that they have been called into *zar* practice during a dream. Kafr el-Elow's only *zar* practitioner claimed to have inherited the role from his grandfather who, in turn, is said to have had a dream wherein he was ordered by a holy man, named Shaik Mahfouz, not only to become a *zar* practitioner, but also to build the *zar* shrine dedicated to Shaik Mahfouz which was referred to earlier in this section.

# 5

# Education: Formal and Informal

## Traditional Education

EDUCATIONAL OPPORTUNITIES in the rural areas of Egypt were extremely limited prior to 1923, when Article XIX of the Egyptian Constitution was passed, stipulating that all boys and girls between the ages of seven and twelve would be provided with free and compulsory elementary schooling. The only school in Kafr el-Elow was the *kuttab* at the mosque, administered by a *shaik* (religious leader) and supported by the villagers; the purpose of the school was, in addition to teaching students to read and write, religious education according to the principles of Islam.

Today, supplementing the secular education, two *shaik* operate *kuttab* in Kafr el-Elow: one at the village mosque, and the other in a rented room near the mosque. The *shaik* receive fees for their educational services from the students' parents, some of whom, as in the past, make their payments in the form of wheat, corn, and other agricultural products. The majority, however, pay cash: from twenty to thirty piasters per month. Most of the students attend irregularly and do so only a few hours each day for a maximum of four years. They regard this educational program as merely supplementary to their schooling at the public school.

At the two *kuttab*, students sit on floor mats in a semicircle around the *shaik*, learning to read and write by copying on black slate tablets passages from the Koran, which they are also expected to memorize. Many boys told me that the *shaik* beat them with a stick when they misbehaved or did not recite their lessons well. Indeed, the *shaik's* punitive treatment of students was evident on the several occasions when I visited the *kuttab*. Moreover, the *shaik* appeared very much on the defensive when I visited their schools, giving the impression that they considered me an intruder and a severe critic of their rural backgrounds and meager educational preparation (elementary school) inasmuch as I was an outsider, a college graduate, urbanite, and non-Moslem.

From 1933, when secular education was first introduced into Kafr el-Elow, until 1950, the public elementary school in the village was conducted in a private home rented by the Ministry of Education. Although a 1933 amendment to Article XIX of the Egyptian Constitution provided that any parents who violated the compulsory school law would be subject to fine and imprisonment, prior to the 1950s the *fellaheen* of Kafr el-Elow, like most Egyptian villagers, never fully accepted the compulsory education system. While at the beginning of each academic year the village school master received from the government a list of all school-age children who should be attending his school, and while the parents of these children were informed of their obligation to send them to school, actual school attendance was extremely poor. Many of those parents who complied with the law and sent their children to the elementary school did so only to escape prosecution, and not more than ten students graduated annually. Ammar, in his book, *Growing Up in an Egyptian Village*, commented as follows on school attendance in Egypt during the 1930s and 1940s:

> The statistics from the Elementary Education Department show that, during the year 1939–1940, average school attendance in the entire country was only about 60 percent of the total number of students registered. Absence from school was especially high in the villages during the irrigation and harvest period when there was much work to be done in the fields. (Ammar 1966:216)

## Modern Education

In 1950, the Portland Cement Company built a second elementary school in Kafr el-Elow for the children of its employees, which became a public school open to all students in the village, when the original public elementary school was closed in 1955 after having been condemned as dilapidated and unsafe. Thereafter, the Ministry of Education in Cairo assumed responsibility for the appointment of the school's two "masters" (principals) and fourteen teachers. When I was in the village, this elementary school offered a six-year education with two daytime shifts: the 7:45–11:45 A.M. period for boys, and the 12:30–4:30 P.M. period for boys and girls.

The square, six-classroom structure is built around a dirt-floored courtyard, where students are lined up by classes after the bell rings for school to begin. There is a drinking fountain in the center of this courtyard. Besides the classrooms, the courtyard leads into the principal's office, the supply room, which serves once a week as an office for the visiting nurse, a room used as a kitchen, and two privies, one for males and one for females. The classrooms, all of which are equipped with electricity, have brick walls covered with whitewash and floors made of cement. Their furnishings consist of a portable blackboard, a map of Egypt and the Middle East, rows of small benches with desks for the students, and a table and chair for the teacher.

In the new public elementary school, the curriculum for the first two years consists of training in the rudiments of the Arabic language, mathematics, music, civics, and physical education. The last four years are devoted to advanced Arabic, religion (Islam), mathematics, social studies, civics, music, natural science, and physical hygiene. A male principal and a staff of seven male teachers operate the school during the first shift each day; during the afternoon session, a female principal and seven female teachers take charge. Only three male teachers, the male principal, and one female teacher reside in Kafr el-Elow; the female principal and the remaining ten teachers reside in Helwan or Cairo and commute to the village every day. All the teachers are between twenty and thirty-five years old, and the two principals are in their forties. The teachers are all high school graduates, with one additional year of education at the Teacher Training Institute in Cairo; the principals have the same amount of formal education, but additional years of teaching experience.

Unfortunately, the new public elementary school has certain disadvantages, one of which is that it constitutes a threat to the students' health because of its location within the cement factory grounds. The classrooms at the back of the school building are adjacent to the cement factory, making it necessary to keep the windows closed at all times, and the students' play area outside the school courtyard is always covered with cement dust. The principal told me that he, the teachers, and the students' parents had requested for several years that the Ministry of Education rectify this situation, but no action had yet been taken. In recent years, however, the labor union at the factory has been accumulating a fund with which to construct a new elementary school at a greater distance from the factory premises. Another major problem confronting the new public elementary school is overcrowded facilities. To alleviate this condition, the school recently inaugurated an evening education program, giving priority to students between the ages of nine and sixteen who cannot be accommodated in the day school. The school principal contended that the quality of the evening education program is not equal to that offered to the day students, for it stresses only the ability to read and write and a basic knowledge of Egyptian history and culture.

### EXTRACURRICULAR FEATURES OF THE VILLAGE ELEMENTARY SCHOOL

Each morning the teachers at the public elementary school inspect their students for cleanliness and those children who fail to meet a reasonable standard in this regard are sent home to their parents. Moreover, each week a nurse visits the school to check on the general health of the students. She is not authorized to administer any medical treatment other than first aid and vaccinations or inoculations. Students in need of more intensive and/or extensive medical care are sent by the nurse to the public health clinic in Helwan, where they are treated free of charge. The school will not re-admit such students until the clinic gives them a clean bill of health. The village school also provides its students with free textbooks and a free daily snack: usually a cup of milk and a cookie or a piece of bread.

Recently, the public elementary school in Kafr el-Elow established a parent-teacher association, but it functions much differently than does the organization in the United States. In Kafr el-Elow, where most of the parents are illiterate, the P.T.A. meeting is never used as an occasion for criticizing teachers. Instead, parents simply inquire about their children's academic progress, express appreciation for the teachers' efforts, and make it clear that they stand behind the instructors, regardless of how they treat the children, as expressed by the Arabic proverb: Take their flesh and give us the bones, if necessary (*khuth il-lahim wa-atinna il-adem*). That teachers are highly respected and even feared in Kafr el-Elow is evidenced by the fact that many parents discipline their children at home by threatening to report their disobedience to the school teacher.

With the villagers' growing awareness of the importance of formal education in occupational success, an increasing number of parents are offering teachers extra compensation in exchange for tutoring their children outside the classroom to hasten their academic progress. Some parents invite their children's teachers to their homes for meals in order to establish a closer relationship with them. Still others send fruits and vegetables to the homes of those teachers who reside in Kafr el-Elow. These presents follow the traditional pattern of gifts given by the parents to the kuttab school teacher; the prime motive behind the parents' generosity being to encourage teachers to take special interest in their children's education.

Each year, the public elementary school takes its students on trips to the archeological museum in nearby Cairo and to the factories around the village in order to make them aware of both the rich historical tradition which they have inherited from their ancestors and of the revolutionary government's industrialization efforts since 1952. Another important academic event sponsored by the elementary school is the stage play (*masrahieh*) presented by the students at the end of each academic year to entertain the villagers.

## Education beyond the Elementary Level

### SECONDARY AND HIGHER EDUCATION

Students who complete their studies at the elementary school in Kafr el-Elow and who pass the government's elementary school examination are eligible to enroll at the secondary school, traveling to nearby Helwan as there is no secondary school in the village. Students who successfully complete secondary school must pass still another government examination in order to become eligible for admission to a state university, their score over and above the passing mark determining which academic program they may pursue.

### TECHNICAL EDUCATION

Youths who fail the government's elementary school examination but who wish to continue their education, must enroll in a technical or vocational school. The increased rate of industrial expansion in Egypt during the past decade has given tremendous impetus to the establishment of more technical schools to train the skilled workers and specialists needed by various factories. The academic program at most technical institutes covers a three-year period. During the first year, theoretical education is emphasized; during the second year, students are permitted to observe the application of the theoretical knowledge learned the previous year; and during the third year, they must apply the theoretical knowledge themselves.

In addition to the technical institutes administered by the Ministry of Education, there are those established by various industries, where preference is given to employees' sons. In 1965, ten youths from Kafr el-Elow were enrolled at the technical institute operated by the iron and steel plant near the village. This school provides free transportation and daily lunch for all its students, and during their third year, gives them money for incidental expenses as well. Upon graduation, the students are guaranteed positions as skilled workers or technicians in the iron and steel plant.

## Formal Education of Females

The formal education of females beyond the elementary level is still extremely rare in the village of Kafr el-Elow, where females constitute less than 20 percent of the student population. Around the age of ten, most girls are expected to help their mothers with the housework and with the care of their younger brothers and sisters. Because this role for most females is generally accepted throughout rural Egypt, most of the villagers feel that extensive formal education would constitute a waste of time, money and effort. I found only one exception to this point of view in the village: a grocer who had sent his daughter to college in Cairo despite strong opposition from his relatives who feared that the girl would become demoralized from exposure to the urban way of life, in spite of the fact that she would be living with her maternal relatives. Moreover, the grocer was extremely proud of the fact that his daughter had become a school teacher upon graduation from college and frequently boasted to me of her accomplishments.

Two factors in the grocer's background may help to explain his liberal views on female education: (1) before moving to Kafr el-Elow for health reasons, he had lived in Cairo for eight years, there coming under the influence of urban values, including those favoring female education, and (2) he had no sons, who are usually a greater source of parental pride than girls, and would therefore receive the extended education. Consistent with the grocer's liberal attitude toward educating his daughter was his failure to resort to the socially approved procedure of taking a second spouse when his wife failed to bear him a son.

The grocer's example, as well as the fact that female teachers have been added recently to the staff of the village elementary school, has had the effect of inducing more villagers to support education for girls, because most parents object to male teachers' coming into contact with their daughters. As indicated previously in this chapter, girls attend only the afternoon session at the elementary school, when the principal and all the teachers are females, although there are boys in their classes.

## The Impact of Formal Education on the Villagers

One of the *kuttab* masters told me that since the mid 1950s the modern public elementary school in the village has assumed increasing responsibility for the basic education of village youths, as indicated in Table 11.

TABLE 11
TOTAL ATTENDANCE AT THE PUBLIC ELEMENTARY SCHOOL
IN KAFR EL-ELOW 1957–1966

| Year | No. of Students in Attendance |
|---|---|
| 1957–58 | 292 |
| 1958–59 | 310 |
| 1959–60 | 320 |
| 1960–61 | 325 |
| 1961–62 | 340 |
| 1962–63 | 346 |
| 1963–64 | 393 |
| 1964–65 | 423 |
| 1965–66 | 480 |

Source: Registrar's File of the Village School for the Years 1957–1966.

This trend is reflected in Tables·12a and 12b, which demonstrate the rising literacy rates in Kafr el-Elow between 1937 and 1960.

TABLE 12a
ILLITERACY AND LITERACY IN KAFR EL-ELOW
(PERSONS UNDER 10 YEARS OF AGE NOT INCLUDED)
MALES

| Educational Level | 1937 | | 1947 | | 1960 | |
|---|---|---|---|---|---|---|
| | NO. | PERCENT | NO. | PERCENT | NO. | PERCENT |
| Illiterate | 960 | 78.4 | 1352 | 76.3 | 1263 | 54.2 |
| Literate | 265 | 21.6 | 421 | 23.7 | 1069 | 45.8 |
| Totals | 1225 | 100.0 | 1773 | 100.0 | 2332 | 100.0 |

Source: U. A. R. Census Book, 1937:37; 1947:45; 1960:150.

TABLE 12b
ILLITERACY AND LITERACY IN KAFR EL-ELOW
(PERSONS UNDER 10 YEARS OF AGE NOT INCLUDED)
FEMALES

| Educational Level | 1937 | | 1947 | | 1960 | |
|---|---|---|---|---|---|---|
| | NO. | PERCENT | NO. | PERCENT | NO. | PERCENT |
| Illiterate | 982 | 93.2 | 1460 | 92.7 | 1918 | 92.1 |
| Literate | 70 | 6.8 | 115 | 7.3 | 164 | 7.9 |
| Totals | 1052 | 100.0 | 1575 | 100.0 | 2082 | 100.0 |

Source: U. A. R. Census Book, 1937:37; 1947:45; 1960:150.

Thus, while males' literacy rate increased a mere 2.1 percent between 1937 and 1947, it increased 22.1 percent btween 1947 and 1960. The fact that females' literacy rate increased only .5 percent percent between 1937 and 1947, and .6 percent between 1947 and 1960 is not surprising in light of the statement made in the previous section that most girls do not complete more than two or three years' education at the elementary school and constitute only 20 percent of the total student population in the village. Moreover, as Tables 12a and 12b indicate, the majority of Kafr el-Elow's population—54.2 percent of the males and 92.1 percent of the females—were still illiterate in 1960. However, these were primarily persons over forty years of age. Whenever I spoke to illiterate villagers about education, they always expressed the wish that they had taken advantage of the educational opportunities available to them when they were younger. As was pointed out in the section on traditional education, school attendance was extremely poor in Kafr el-Elow prior to 1950. The illiterate villagers' recent expression of interest in formal education seems to suggest, that the public elementary school in Kafr el-Elow has made a significant impact during the last decade.

By 1960, nine people in Kafr el-Elow—eight men and one woman (the grocer's daughter referred to in the previous section)—had obtained a college degree and/or post graduate education (see Table 13). All these individuals were lifelong residents of the village, not recent immigrants.

When this study was completed in 1966, thirteen students from the village were attending various colleges and universities. Assuming that all thirteen complete their college programs and graduate by the end of 1968, there will have been almost a seventy percent increase (from nine in 1960 to thirteen in 1968) in the number of college graduates in the village since 1960. Inasmuch as education is the key to higher status employment in Kafr el-Elow, as is true everywhere in the world, this remarkable increase in the educational attainment level of its population should contribute to the acceleration of the trend toward increasing intergenerational mobility in the village, as was discussed in Chapter II.

## The Mass Media

Anyone visiting Kafr el-Elow for the first time is impressed by the large number of villagers listening to music and news on their transistor radios. Every-

TABLE 13
HIGHER EDUCATION IN KAFR EL-ELOW, 1960

| Educational Level | Males | Females |
|---|---|---|
| University or College Degree | 6 | 1 |
| Post-Graduate Diploma | 2 | 0 |
| Master's Degree | 0 | 0 |
| Ph.D. Degree | 0 | 0 |
| Totals | 8 | 1 |

Source: *U. A. R. Census Book*, 1960:150.

where I went in the village—to the grocery store, to private homes, to the barber shop, to the vegetable peddler sitting in the street—I encountered a transistor radio operating at full volume. Many factory workers and field hands in the village carry transistor radios to work. Most of the villagers who own transistor radios buy them in Helwan or else they purchase them in Kafr el-Elow from a school teacher who operates a small radio and watch repair shop in the evenings. The teacher actually takes watches and radios in need of repair to a dealer in Helwan, pocketing a certain percentage of the repair fee.

He told me that since 1960, when he opened his part-time business, the villagers had purchased over 500 radios, most of which had been sold on a credit basis: that is, with the customer making a small down payment and a succession of weekly payments thereafter. One day the teacher asked me to accompany him as he went about the village collecting payments. In one case, he took two five-pound packages of meat from a butcher who owed him money and subtracted the value thereof from the butcher's indebtedness. I was told by the teacher after this visit that whenever the butcher could not meet his weekly payments for the radio he had purchased, he (the teacher) simply took meat of equivalent value and sold it to friends in Helwan.

While television may be viewed in Kafr el-Elow, it is not nearly as important as the radio as a popular means of communication. There were only six television sets in the village while I was there, all of which were purchased after my arrival in 1964. Since the owners of these television sets occasionally invite relatives, friends, and neighbors to their homes to view certain programs, the influence of television on the villagers' attitudes and behavior is much more widespread than the small number of sets would seem to indicate. One young man in the village told me that he had doubted most of what he had been told about city life in Cairo until he saw various aspects of it portrayed in television programs emanating from that city, where the first televison station was established in 1959.

Newspapers and magazines cannot be purchased in Kafr el-Elow, but they may be obtained in nearby Helwan and Cairo. I frequently saw elderly and illiterate men bring newspapers several days old to a village barber or tailor shop, hoping to find someone there who would be willing to read the paper aloud so that they might learn what was going on in the world. Many people in Kafr el-Elow express a keen interest in obtaining news of national and international events, but the major means of fulfilling this desire are still person-to-person contact and, increasingly, the radio. A conversation which I overheard one market day between two elderly villagers—a grain merchant and his customer—clearly illustrates this fact. When the customer asked the grain merchant if he had any yellow corn (American corn) to sell, the latter impatiently replied: "Where have you been, *fellah*? Don't you listen to the radio? Whenever the Americans get mad at us, they stop sending yellow corn. So, fellow citizen, get used to the idea of eating white corn (Egyptian corn), and never depend on the Americans."[1] When I asked the merchant about his source of information concerning the American embargo on corn shipments to Egypt, the old man pointed to his transistor radio.

---

[1] Exports of American surplus corn were halted for awhile in 1965 as the result of a speech made that year by President Nasser attacking American foreign policy in the Middle East.

The late President Nasser has commented as follows on the importance of the radio as a means of issuing daily news to the widely diffused social and geographic segments of the Egyptian population:

> It is true that most of our people are still illiterate. But, politically, that counts far less than it did twenty years ago . . . Radio has changed everything. . . . Today people in the most remote villages hear of what is happening everywhere and form their opinions. Leaders cannot govern as they once did; we live in a new world. (Lerner 1958:214)

The following quotation, which expresses the significant impact on the village population of Egypt, of the mass media in general as well as of formal education, is especially relevant to this chapter's discussion of formal and informal education in Kafr el-Elow:

> Today, villagers are definitely emerging as a nationally conscious group. Strongly associated with this development is the role of the mass media, super-imposed upon traditional word-of-mouth communication. Our research has also indicated a relationship between literacy and political sophistication. If it is true that literacy is increasing with the spread of public elementary and secondary schools, then political awareness in the village should also increase. Coupled with the increasing availability and effectiveness of the mass media, political awareness (even to international consciousness) seems destined to spread among the villagers. (Hirabayashi and Khatib 1956:363)

# 6

# Village Government

## The Traditional Government

PRIOR TO THE 1960s, the government of Kafr el-Elow, like that of most Egyptian villages, was largely based on kinship structure. Each *hamula* (clan) in a village nominated four persons for the position of *shaik*. Only one of the four persons nominated by each clan was selected by the Ministry of Interior Affairs for the position of *shaik*, with the obvious result that the total number of *shaik* elected was equal to the number of clans in the village. Since small families in the village frequently joined large clans in associations called *houssa* (share), each elected *shaik* usually represented, for official business purposes, several families: his own clan, plus all the smaller families aligned with it. Since the *shaik's* positions were honorary, they received no salary for performing their role.

The *shaik* were supervised by, and were under the authority of, the *omda*, whose position was legally defined in 1895 as official representative of the central government to the village *fellaheen*. The *omda* was selected from a list of candidates submitted by all the villagers, by a commission from the Ministry of Interior Affairs called *lagnat il-Shiyakhat*, but his official appointment had to be approved by the Minister of Interior Affairs himself, who also had the power to dismiss the *omda* and to appoint a new one, if this became necessary. In order to be considered for the position of *omda*, a candidate had to own no fewer than five feddan, to be less than sixty years old, and to be able to read and write. In addition to being popular with the villagers, the *omda* had to come from a distinguished and affluent family, since his position required him to entertain guests and government officials on numerous occasions (Ammar 1966:61). In many villages, the *omda's* position was traditionally limited to a particular family, being transmitted from father to son for several generations. The post of the *omda* in Kafr el-Elow was originally filled by members of the Darwish clan, but then the responsibility shifted to the Dawudeya clan, where it lay till the position was abolished by the government in 1960.

Traditionally, the *omda* and his subordinate *shaik* constituted the sole government authority in Kafr el-Elow, as they did in many Egyptian villages, functioning in a largely protective capacity. Not only did they settle internal village disputes, but they also supervised the guards (*ghafeer*), whose duty it was to protect the community, especially at night, from vagabonds and thieves. The *omda* possessed the judicial power to arrest law violators apprehended by these guards and to turn them over to the nearest *markaz* (police headquarters) in Helwan. The central government in Cairo installed a telephone in the home of the *omda* to facilitate his communicating with the police station. Still another function served by the *omda* and his *shaik* was the supervision of the village census: the reporting of births, deaths, and epidemics. The *shaik* also prepared a list of names from their respective *houssa* of all males who had reached draft age, and they were expected to accompany the tax collector (*sarraf*) into the fields to collect taxes from land cultivators. In return for performing these functions, the sons of *omda* and *shaik* were excused from military service.

The prestige of the *omda's* and *shaik's* positions in Kafr el-Elow and in other rural areas of Egypt gradually declined after 1952, a trend explained by Ammar as follows:

> The *omda* of the village is elected on the basis of his land property, and has been the symbol of authority and responsibility on behalf of the village. Now, with the establishment of a police station, with the availability of more people who can write out complaints, with the decrease in the wealth of the village *omda*, and, consequently, with his inability to provide hospitality in the traditional way, or to represent the village properly without extending his hands for help from the village, his authority has been flouted and people tend to send their complaints and disputes directly to the police station or to the provincial authorities. They complain that the *omda* is not what he used to be in the good old days—responsible for the reception and accommodation of government officials and generous to chance travelers and to the needy poor. (Ammar 1966:80)

Other factors that contributed to the decline of the *omda's* position were the economic and political reforms implemented by the revolutionary government.

## The Modern Government

At present, Kafr el-Elow is under the direct jurisdiction of the subadministrative district (*Kism*) of Helwan, which is in charge of the southern part of the Cairo Governorate and is directly connected with the office of the Governor (*Mouhafiz*) of the Cairo Governorate (*Mouha-Fazit il-Kahira*). Consequently, the *fellaheen* of Kafr el-Elow now conduct most of their business in Helwan. Routine security in the village and its neighboring areas is maintained by a police station which was esablished in 1960 in Kafr el-Elow. Located at the extreme east side of the village in a couple of rooms contributed by the cement factory, the station is administered by a police lieutenant who commutes daily from Helwan, and in his absence a police sergeant takes charge. Cases which the lieutenant or sergeant cannot handle, or which are beyond their jurisdiction, are relayed by telephone to police headquarters in Helwan.

The village guards (*ghafeer*), who were part of the traditional government system in Kafr el-Elow, still exist, but they are now directly connected with the police station rather than with the *omda*. The eighteen *ghafeer* in Kafr el-Elow come not only from the village, but also from neighboring areas. Some work the day shift; others are active during the night shift. At the beginning of each shift, the guards report to the police station to get their rifles, and at the end of the shift, they report back to the station to turn in their weapons. Since the *ghafeer* wear the standard village clothing (the *jalabiya*), the rifle is their only distinguishing feature. The ordinary *ghafeer* is paid between six and seven Egyptian pounds per month, while the head *ghafeer*, who is in charge of the shift, receives between seven and nine Egyptian pounds per month.

After the abolishment of the traditional government system in Kafr el-Elow in 1960, a new administrative position was created: that of the *shaik il-balad*, whose administrative responsibilities extend beyond the village to two nearby settlements. The Ministry of Interior Affairs appoints the *shaik il-balad*, whose monetary compensation is about twelve Egyptian pounds per month. The man holding the office of *shaik il-balad* in Kafr el-Elow originally came from a small and socioeconomically insignificant family in the village, and was an officer in the secret police (*moukhabarat*) at Port Said for twenty years prior to assuming this position.

The new position of *shaik il-balad* incorporates some of the same responsibilities as those formerly performed by the *omda* and his *shaik* in the village. For example, the *shaik il-balad* now accompanies the village tax agent as he collects taxes from the *fellaheen*; he prepares a list of draft-eligible men which he submits to the government and notifies the men thereon to report for duty; he certifies identification cards; he informs villagers about new government regulations; and he summons those whom the government authorities in Helwan wish to see for investigatory or other purposes. Unlike the former *omda* and *shaik*, however, the *shaik il-balad* does not solve village disputes. For this reason, he experiences tremendous difficulty in performing his role, because the villagers expect him to help them solve their problems in the same way as did the former *omda* and *shaik*. If he refuses, the villagers ostracize him and, if he accedes to their requests, his supervisors accuse him of accepting bribes from the villagers. Kafr el-Elow's *shaik il-balad* told me that he had twice applied to his supervisor for a transfer, but his request had been refused both times.

## The New Political Horizon

Until recently, the *fellaheen* in Egypt were generally regarded as living an isolated existence in their respective village communities. Ammar has explained their traditional situation in the following words:

> It is appropriate to mention that, in spite of the political and social vicissitudes which overtook Egyptian society, folk life held its own, oftentimes against trends in the larger society. Various political struggles have occurred throughout the history of Egypt, but the common people, tied down to their land, submitted to any social order enforced upon them. They rarely took part in any resistance and left the battles to the military and ruling classes. (Ammar 1966:70)

Indeed, prior to 1952, Egypt's social structure was dominated by a small class, most of whom were wealthy landowners. With the 1952 Revolution, however, this old political order was abolished in favor of a liberal constitutional government.

The villagers' awareness and understanding of the political changes which have swept their country since the advent of the Nasser regime are expressed by their recognition and use of such terms as *ishtirakiya* (socialism), *huriya* (freedom), *adala* (justice), *ilqwmiya* (nationalism), and *il-istimar* (imperialism) which the government employs frequently in the mass media and in signs hung at entrances to factories, hospitals, and schools. The villagers would have no interest in these abstract political principles, however, if the government were not characterized by "good works," which they define in such terms as employment for themselves and education for their children, both of which bring them greater security and dignity. Under the late President Nasser, the Egyptian *fellaheen* and industrial workers have also been given the privilege of voting freely for the first time in the history of the country.

As social reforms have progressed, the *fellaheen* of Kafr el-Elow, like those in most Egyptian villages, have become more conscious of their role within the society and, concomitantly, have gradually developed feelings of nationhood and state sovereignty. Undoubtedly, many of the *fellaheen* had been skeptical about the sincerity of the revolutionary government for a long time, but while some of them probably still are, this feeling has all but disappeared, especially in Kafr el-Elow due to its proximity to Cairo and the availability of industrial work near the village. The great majority of the *fellaheen* seem convinced that the Cairo government wants to help rather than to exploit them as did the earlier tradition-bound regimes. Kerr has described the most recent developments in Egyptian socialism as follows:

> It was not until 1960 that "socialism" began to take on a more definite ideological character, marked by explanations of a semi-Marxist tone. These explanations foreshadowed the more developed doctrines accompanying the sweeping decrees of July 19–23, 1960, which transferred to state ownership or control virtually all economic enterprises except those of small shopkeepers, artisans and farmers, wiped out large incomes, and transformed the character of the Egyptian economy from one of mixed, but still extensively private ownership, to one of thoroughgoing socialism. (Kerr 1962:127–131)

The importance of the mass media—especially radios—and formal education in the dissemination of these modern socio-economic doctrines was discussed in the previous chapter.

Another significant agency contributing to the political modernization of Egypt is the *Itihad il-Arabi il-ishtiraki*, the Arab Socialist Union Party, which is the only party permitted to function in the country. Members of the agricultural cooperatives in the village are automatically affiliated with the party, as are factory workers through the trade unions at their places of employment. Consequently, the various trade unions perform the important function of orienting the *fellaheen* to desire social equality: before the establishment of the Arab Socialist Union Party, the *fellaheen* had never been courted by political officials or parties. Another factor which brought the villagers of Kafr el-Elow closer to modern political institutions was the abolition of their traditional government, making it necessary for them to deal directly with the central government in Cairo.

## The Settlement of Disputes

### *Urf* LAW (CUSTOMARY LAW)

In Kafr el-Elow, as in rural Egypt generally, *urf* law is still the most influential means by which villagers attempt to resolve their grievances, whether the issue is as serious as murder or as trifling as an insult or swearing. *Urf* law is the unwritten law that was used by Arab tribes prior to the rise of Islam which has been passed down orally from one generation to another and is unofficially accepted by the civil authorities. *Il hukum il-ashairi, ada,* and *hag il-arab* are other terms used in different parts of the Arab Middle East to refer to *urf* law. The fact that tribal organization still dominates the social structure in the rural areas of the Middle East largely accounts for the persistence of *urf* law in the Arab world (Hardy 1963:47–73; Lutfiyya 1966:92–100; Abou Zaid 1963:301–361).

According to *urf* law, each member of a clan is responsible for the welfare of all the other members, in return for which he receives assistance and protection from his clan. Vulnerability to death, physical harm, or social penalties for violations of *urf* law also has a collective character in that any member of the aggressor clan may be killed in reprisal for the acts of a kinsman. However, the immediate kin of an injured person always have the option of accepting monetary compensation (*diyya*) through the tribal court in lieu of physical revenge, especially if the injury was inflicted unintentionally (Hardy 1963:11).

Murder can become a critical problem, especially when inter-clan feuds continue for years. *The Al-Mussawar Journal* reported one case of a blood feud starting in 1951 and ending in 1966, during which time 295 members of two clans were killed as the result of *thar*: the revenge which each family tried to inflict on the other (*Al-Mussawar Journal*, November 18, 1966:9). In 1963, *The National Review of Criminal Science* reported that 34.8 percent of all murders committed in Egypt during that year were blood revenge murders (*The National Review of Criminal Science*, Vol. VI, 1963:301), so the blood feud mentioned above can hardly be considered unique.

While strong kinship bonds, which are the motivating force behind blood revenge murders, are as prominent a phenomenon in the village of Kafr el-Elow as they are in other Egyptian villages, blood feuds are not common here. Village informants said that only one case of blood feud had occurred in the village— during the year 1940—but its impact was still being felt by some members of both clans involved.

### THE TRIBAL COURT—*Majliss il-urfi*

Whenever a conflict arises, regardless of its type or cause, several elderly and prominent men in the village usually interfere to freeze hostilities by suggesting that the case be referred to the *majliss il-urfi* for settlement. The injured party then nominates three houses as potential sites for the hearing, one of which is to be chosen by the offender. If the offender refuses to accept any of the three, however, members of the *majliss* nominate several houses from which the two conflicting parties select one that is mutually acceptable.

After an agreement has been reached concerning the place for the hearing, the *majliss* determines the amount of the *rizka* or *sutra*. This is the money paid to the owner of the home agreed upon as the site for the hearing, the amount varying according to the nature of the case and the number of people invited to observe the proceedings and to serve as witnesses: usually, the heads of prominent families in the village and a few people from neighboring villages. Especially in cases of blood feud, the police commissioner or the governor of the *mouhafaza* may be invited to attend the *majliss il-urfi*. The *rizka* money is expected to cover all the expenses for food and entertainment incurred by the host, plus serve as compensation for his efforts at offering hospitality. Both parties in the conflict under investigation give *rizka* money to their host before the hearing takes place, but after the hearing the loser forfeits his contribution, while the winner receives a refund.

The number of members constituting the *majliss* for a particular case, as well as the mode of their selection, depends upon the nature of the conflict to be settled. Most commonly, both parties in the dispute select the members of the *majliss* by choosing an equal number from their two lists of nominees. The judges selected in this manner then meet to decide upon another judge whose role will become especially important if the original members reach a deadlock in attempting to settle a case. Objectivity is considered an essential attribute of all members of the *majliss*; indeed, their reputations are seriously impaired if they fail to maintain impartiality in every case. Unjust behavior is condemned by the Koran in the following verses:

> O believers, be you securers of justice, witnesses for God, even though it be against yourselves, or your parents and kinsmen, whether the man be rich or poor; God stands closest to either. Then follow not caprice, so as to swerve; for if you twist or turn, God is aware of the things you do. (Koran, 4:134–135)

On the date set for the hearing by the heads of the disputants' clans, both they and any other kin who may be involved in the case meet with members of the *majliss* and invited guests at the designated site. After both the accused and the accuser swear on the Koran that they will not give false information to members of the *majliss*, their testimony is heard and members of the *majliss* interrogate them to clarify certain points. Then the *majliss* adjourns to another room to arrive at a verdict; if the alleged offender is found guilty, a decision is made regarding the amount of money which he should pay the offended party.

Before publicly announcing its verdict, the *majliss* informs the heads of both disputants' clan of its decision in the case. Moreover, if a fine is imposed, the amount announced publicly by the *majliss* is always larger than that which has been agreed upon privately, because guests at the hearing generally prevail upon the offended party's family to reduce the amount of money which they will demand from the offender's clan in honor of the governor of the *mouhafaza*, President Nasser, or some other person. The *majliss* usually assigns a *kafeel* "co-signer" to each of the disputants to make certain that the verdict is executed, the persons performing this role are prominent residents of the village who have been nominated and selected by both parties in the case. The verdict is usually executed without complications, but should any member of either disputant's family or clan challenge the *majliss'* decision, he would be publicly ostracized from his clan and no longer given support or protection in time of need.

At the conclusion of the hearing, the offender and the offended shake hands, kiss each other's heads, and swear on the Koran that they will forget what has happened. Then the guests, members of the *majliss*, and the parties involved in the case all join together in eating a meal which their host has prepared. According to Islamic belief, the judges constituting the *majliss*, and consequently playing the mediator role (*waseet*) in the solution of disputes, will be rewarded by Allah. They also achieve high status and respect in the villages where they live for this part in restoring harmonious relationships between individuals and families.

## SOME ILLUSTRATIVE CASES

CASE I   In the past, villagers frequently slept in their fields during the summer months to protect their crops from thieves, those owning adjacent fields usually gathering each evening to socialize and drink tea. On these occasions, one would get water for the tea, another would collect pieces of wood for the fire with which to boil the water, and another would prepare the tea. In one of these situations, a fellow who was supposed to prepare tea asked another in his group to get some wood and start a fire; when the latter did not respond immediately, the former tried to attract his attention by pointing a gun at him in a joking manner. Unfortunately, however, the gun accidentally went off and killed the man. Subsequently, the relatives of the slain man gathered to avenge his killing.

According to *urf* law, a victim's clan is given a three-and-a-third day cooling-off period, known as *foratid-dam* (the boiling of the blood), during which to retaliate against the offender's clan in any way they see fit; if they fail to take advantage of this privilege, they must abide by the settlement terms decided upon by the *majliss il-urfi*. In this case, the slain man's clan did take advantage of their cooling-off period, killing the livestock and burning the crops of the offender's clan to inflict economic harm upon them and to tempt them to come out of their homes to fight. When the offender's father finally did leave his home, several members of the slain man's clan beat him to death. The blood feud between the two clans ended at that point as the debt had been paid in full: a life for a life; consequently, there was no need for the *majliss il-urfi* to render a decision in the case.

CASE II   The conflict started when a boy from Clan A was caught stealing hay from the field of a man from Clan B, whereupon the owner of the field beat the boy and then released him.[1] When the boy told his father about the thrashing he had received, the latter went to the field and retaliated by striking the owner. Subsequently, the field owner went to the village to report his beating to the members of his clan, several of whom ganged upon the boy's father and beat him as he

---

[1] Capital letters have been substituted for actual names in the interest of confidentiality.

was returning from the field. From that point on, news rapidly spread that several members of Clans A and B had beat one another, and soon both clans became involved in a battle that resulted in injury to twelve persons. No one was fatally injured, however, as leaders from other clans eventually interfered to stop the fighting. And, the heads of the two clans finally decided to settle the case through *urf* law. The verdict ultimately arrived at and reported by a Bedouin chief from a neighboring Bedouin village was a fine of 100 Egyptian pounds to be paid by Clan B to Clan A as compensation for the boy's beating, even though he had been caught stealing. The rationale behind the council's decision was that the field owner should have reported the stealing incident to the boy's father, rather than beating the boy. In addition, Clan B was made liable for the *rizka* expenses (50 Egyptian pounds).

CASE III   This conflict arose when a fellow from Clan C was caught stealing from the field of a fellow from Clan D and was beaten by the owner. Several days later, the thief waited for the fellow who had given him the beating and hit him on the head without warning. Some more prudent individuals interfered in the case, however, with the result that the head of Clan C requested that a representative from Clan D meet with him to settle the issue through the *urf* council. The thief was fined fifty Egyptian pounds plus the *rizka* money. The council penalized the thief in this case because he was an adult, in contrast with Case II, where the offender was shown indulgence because he was a child.

CASE IV   This was an inter-family feud which originated when two brothers agreed that their offspring (one's daughter and the other's son) should marry; in other words, they arranged a paternal-cousin marriage between their children. According to informants, when the boy's mother realized that her son had entered the marriage against his will, she tried to terminate the union by poisoning her daughter-in-law's food but her son ate the poisoned food by mistake. Following the young man's death, his parents and in-laws fought continuously. Finally, when the dead man's mother accused his surviving wife and mother-in-law of stealing some of her gold jewelry, the fathers of both families agreed to settle the case through the *urf* council. Each contributed a *rizka* of fifty Egyptian pounds to the family whose home and dining facilities would be used during the hearing. Only fifteen persons (including the writer), all prominent and respected people in Kafr el-Elow, were invited to the *mandara* of the home where the hearing was held. The *urf* council opened the hearing by reading the *Fatiha*. Next, the fathers of the conflicting families were asked to raise their hands and swear on the Koran that their testimony would be truthful. The judges then asked the father whose daughter and wife had been accused of stealing the gold jewelry to go with a witness to an adjacent room in order to administer the same oath to the defendants, since females are not ordinarily permitted to appear before strange men. When the man objected, insisting that his wife and daughter be brought into the *mandara* to swear before all who were present at the hearing that they were innocent of the charge, the judges complied with his wish. The judges then asked the accusers if they were convinced that the defendants' testimony was true. After the accusers indicated that they were satisfied, the judges requested that both brothers embrace and kiss each other and swear on the Koran that they would forgive one another and forget their grievances. Shortly thereafter, rice, meat, and bread were served to those attending the hearing. Since the host, a maternal relative of both brothers, had been especially anxious to help solve this case, he attempted to return the fifty pound hospitality fee which each of the brothers had contributed, but the husband of the plaintiff refused to accept his share. Following the meal, the guests proceeded for tea to the houses of the two families who had just settled their differences, and both brothers visited one another's home for the first time in three years.

CASE V   This case involved three men who were employed by the Iron and Steel Factory in Kafr el-Elow, two of whom were natives, while the third was a newcomer to the village. One day, the two native men went to visit a roomer at the house where the newcomer lived. When persistent knocking and shouting failed to elicit a response, the two men went to the second floor of the house where they found the newcomer sitting on the top step of the stairway overlooking the court-yard of the building. The newcomer became very hostile about this invasion of his privacy and proceeded to insult the visitors with offensive language. After the two men had left; he discovered that both came from large and prominent families in the village and began to fear for his safety. Consequently, he went immediately to *Markaz il-Subak*, a village near Kafr el-Elow where he had been reared, and asked three prominent persons to accompany him to the homes of the two men whom he had insulted in order to arrange for an *urf* council so that he might pay damages. The heads of the offended families agreed to waive a hearing in the case and accepted the offending man's apologies, telling his supporters that since he had admitted his error, they would absolve him from the obligation of paying a fine. They warned the defendant, however, that if he ever repeated the offense, a stringent penalty would be imposed upon him.

## A FINAL COMMENTARY ON *Urf* LAW IN KAFR EL-ELOW

One of the most important factors contributing to the infrequent occurrence of interpersonal and interfamily disputes in Kafr el-Elow is the relative homogeneity of the villagers' socioeconomic condition, reducing the tendency for one clan to dominate another. However, this social equality among the *fella-heen* in Kafr el-Elow means that whenever a murder or some other serious crime is committed, the status of the victim's family or clan will rapidly deteriorate if they fail to avenge his death or injury, for an act of aggression against one clan member is considered an act of aggression against the entire clan. Clan members who disregard this obligation are referred to by such shameful labels as *hareem* (females), not *rejalla* (males).

It is not necessary that the victim's clan retaliate against the offender himself; a prominent member of the latter's family may be selected for reprisal purposes. Women and children, however, are not regarded as suitable targets for revenge. Moreover, a murdered person's kin usually prefer to take revenge themselves rather than to provide information to government officials which might lead to the offender's arrest because life imprisonment is generally the most severe penalty meted out by the government for murder, in which case the offender may live more comfortably than he would at home. Instead, they attempt to confuse the government's law enforcement authorities by accusing a member of the offender's clan who they know is not guilty, with the result that the case is soon closed and labeled unsolved. In other words, most clans take tremendous pride in their ability to settle any dispute involving one of their members without calling upon civil authorities.

## THE CIVIL COURTS

Today, Islamic Law and the religious courts operate side-by-side with the civil law and civil courts in Egypt, each dealing with specific types of cases. The religious courts, are generally limited to divorce, marriage, and inheritance cases, while the civil courts handle all other types of investigations. However, the foregoing discussion demonstrated clearly that villagers in general do not rely upon civil authority to settle disputes. Several of the village elders in Kafr el-Elow told me that only persons without backbone resort to the civil courts in such cases. This statement reflects the importance of *urf* law in maintaining group solidarity, for cases settled by a civil court involve only the few individuals who are directly involved, while those which are settled by *urf* law involve two or more entire clans as well as government officials such as the district police commissioner and the governor of the *mouhafaza*, especially when homicide or rape has been committed.

V. Ayoub, in an article entitled "Conflict Resolution and Social Reorganization in a Lebanese Village," explains the Arabian villagers' tendency to choose adjudicating procedures consistent with the indigenous social structure rather than those employed by the central government's courts:

> For the Lebanese villager, appeal to an agency of the state is not a viable alternative. Recognition that the authority of the state is alien and, therefore, to be feared is not likely to promote a genuine choice. . . . [Moreover,] an individual who resorts to the courts does not solve the problem of the group, whatever the result of the court action. The need for mediation persists, because reconciliation of the disputants continues to be considered important in maintaining the solidarity of the group. . . . Thus, appeal to the courts not only does not eliminate or supersede the mediation procedure, but makes the success of the latter more difficult to achieve. It is not surprising, then, that there is considerable resistance to the use of courts. Nevertheless, the alternative is there, and some have chosen it. The choice reflects a process of transformation in important social relationships affecting village life. (Ayoub 1964:11–13)

Despite the villagers' general reluctance to have recourse to the civil courts in settling their disputes, the social structure in Kafr el-Elow is changing. I was informed by the officer in charge of the police station that more villagers, especially newcomers, are submitting their grievances and other problems to civil authorities, rather than resorting to the traditional methods. The following are the major factors accounting for this new orientation:

1. Since 1960, when a police station was established in Kafr el-Elow, the villagers have had a greater sense of physical and psychological security. Prior to this time, the nearest police station was that located in Helwan, and it was too remote to be considered an effective law-enforcement agency for the village.
2. With the replacement of the traditional village government (the *omda* and his staff) by a civilian officer (*shaik il-balad*) who serves as a liaison officer

between the district (*kism*) headquarters in Helwan and Kafr el-Elow, the villagers have found it necessary to go to Helwan to conduct most of their official business, because the *shaik il-balad* will not perform as many services for them as did the previous regime.

3. The influx of migrants who have come to work in the various industries surrounding the village has introduced new values into the community which have especially affected kinship structure. With the rising prominence of materialistic values, for example, the traditional approach to settling disputes, which tends to be expensive not only for those directly involved but also for their entire clans, is being modified so that each family within a clan is financially responsible only for disputes involving its immediate members (*ahl il-lazam*).

4. The mass media, such as transistor radios, television, and newspapers, are acquainting the villagers with the urban standard of living.

As a consequence of these social forces, the villagers have become less reluctant to solve a variety of problems using the new methods, most of which are more formal and impersonal than were the traditional systems. In other words, urban ways are regarded with less suspicion as the villagers' contact with large urban centers increases. As a result, the villagers now have a greater choice of machinery to use in settling disputes.

# 7

# Summary and Conclusions

WHEN I CAME to Kafr el-Elow in 1964 and proposed that the results of my research in the village during the next two years would benefit the Egyptian government, other Arab states, and Middle Eastern scholars, the villagers were somewhat apprehensive. I was the first researcher they had ever encountered. Moreover, they were surprised that any stranger would be sincerely interested in studying their daily activities and efforts to improve their own socioeconomic conditions. When the villagers learned that I had been reared in the Arab world they gradually relaxed and became less reticent about discussing various aspects of their life which have been described in the preceding chapters.

As was stated in the introductory section, the village of Kafr el-Elow was chosen for an ethnographic study not only because of its proximity to Cairo, but also because of its location in the midst of Egypt's largest industrial complex, making it possible to study the impact of the urbanization and industrialization processes on the traditional way of life. This was accomplished mainly by means of participant observation, interviewing, and case history analysis.

When I was in Kafr el-Elow, a very definite struggle for dominance was being waged between the new industrial and the traditional agricultural economic orders, as a consequence of which the old social order was not only undergoing modification, but also, in some areas, a complete transformation. The average villager was quite literally living in two different worlds: an urban-industrial realm during the day, and a folk-agricultural realm during the nonworking hours. The study clearly demonstrates that today's life in Kafr el-Elow is different from that of yesterday, and tomorrow's will be different from today's. Nevertheless, although the many social and economic changes described here have already occurred in Kafr el-Elow and many are currently in progress, their full impact and repercussions have yet to be realized.

116

# The Community of Kafr el-Elow in Retrospect

As was pointed out earlier in this study, the village of Kafr el-Elow was established by six families who came to this area seventeen miles south of Cairo in the mid-eighteenth century. In time, the original six families multiplied to produce six distinct kinship groups; these, in turn, intermarried and further increased the population. Eventually, other families migrated to the village causing its population to reach 6608 persons by 1960. As the population increased, the social structure or organization of the village became more complex, leading to the development of a very definite community consciousness among the inhabitants.

From the time when Kafr el-Elow came in to existence to the time when this study came to an end in 1966, the village community passed through three distinct stages. The first stage, which commenced with the establishment of the village, lasted nearly 150 years: up to the early 1900s. During this period the village was a small homogeneous community, the economy of which was based on subsistence farming, the *fellaheen* raising annual crops, such as wheat, corn, beans, and cotton, mainly for their own consumption. (A small portion of the cotton was usually sold, however, to obtain money for purchasing basic family commodities such as gasoline for home lighting, sugar, and tea.) Since crop cultivation was a family effort, kinship bonds were very strong. According to several elderly informants in the village, the residents of Kafr el-Elow resembled one big clan prior to the beginning of the twentieth century. Despite their proximity to Cairo and Helwan, most of the villagers lived in complete isolation because no paved roads connected Kafr el-Elow with these two cities. The few who left the village occasionally to visit or shop in Helwan were forced to walk or ride a donkey or a horse.

During the first stage of its history, Kafr el-Elow's only permanent link with the central government in Cairo was the *omda*, the chief figure of authority in the village. While the tax collector also represented the central government, his contact with the villagers was limited to visits once or twice a year. Moreover, his image was one of oppression rather than benevolence, due to the fact that he collected taxes imposed upon the villagers without their consent. The only formal education available in Kafr el-Elow during this period was that offered in the *kuttab*, a religious school administered and operated by the shaik of the village mosque. The primary objective of this education was to teach male youngsters to memorize the Koran.

The second stage of Kafr el-Elow's history began in the early 1920s when a few pieces of modern machinery were introduced into the village, the first being the government water pump, which was used for irrigation. Another innovation of equal significance which occurred about this time was the establishment of the village cement factory and textile mill. Economic gains from the new industrial technology were small and limited, however, because only a few villagers were engaged in factory work and this was on a seasonal basis. After a gravel road linking Kafr el-Elow with Helwan and Cairo was constructed in the mid 1930s, once-a-day bus service became available to the villagers. Secular education was also introduced to Kafr el-Elow during the 1930s, and despite the fact that the villagers were not initially conscientious about sending their children to the public school, a new trend was established which has gradually but significantly increased the literacy rate of the village population.

The second stage of Kafr el-Elow's history came to an end early in the 1950s after a decade of exposure to the influences of World War II. During this period many of the villagers had come into contact with foreigners for the first time, had gained greater familiarity with the urban way of life, had become acquainted with new types of industrial machinery, and had been engaged in a variety of war-time occupations which created several new sources of income in the village. The Revolution of 1952, initiating a new political, social, and economic order in Egypt, marked the beginning of the third stage of Kafr el-Elow's history. As was pointed out earlier in this study, Egypt's largest industrial complex started rising in the Helwan area during the late 1950s, producing marked changes in the social and economic life of the community.

Chapter 3 discussed kinship organization in Kafr el-Elow, which is characterized by four components: patrilineal descent, patrilocal residence, patriarchal authority, and preferred kin group endogamy. Kinship ties are not limited to the nuclear family; on the contrary, they are extensive, producing a network of social relations among relatives that makes the kinship group a clearly distinguishable unit within the village. Clans are strongly united when the reputation of the village is at stake or when the village community feels threatened by outsiders. This solidarity may be attributed not only to the common place of residence, but also to a cohesive network of social relationships based on intermarriage which has prevailed since the time when the village community was established. The terms *amam* and *akhwal*, commonly used by older villagers when speaking about their identity as members of the village community, mean "we are all paternal and maternal uncles," and reflect the fact that the social solidarity among members of different clans is primarily based on kinship. This network of interclan relationships has been frequently compared with an elastic rope in the sense that it can withstand considerable strain—stretching and pulling by extraneous factors—without being broken. Many elderly informants told me that even though competition and friction exist both within and between clans, if an outsider were to threaten any of the native villagers, all clan members would put aside their internal and external difficulties in order to confront the stranger together.

The strong sense of social solidarity among the long-established clans in Kafr el-Elow is also expressed by the impersonal character of their interaction with newcomers who have moved to the village in recent years. As a result, newcomers patronize almost exclusively businesses owned and operated by newcomers. For example, most of the customers of the modern barber who moved from Helwan in 1960 are newcomers; only lately have a few native villagers—mostly young people—started to patronize him. The traditional village barber, on the other hand, is still patronized mainly by native villagers and by only a few newcomers. When newcomers patronize native businesses, they are always given the prices specified by the government, while the owners tend to hike prices for natives. Native businessmen fear that newcomers may be government inspectors or that they would report being overcharged to government officials.

That older natives also identify very strongly with the village of Kafr el-Elow itself is expressed by the familiar statement, *sukan il-balad il asleeyiin* (we are the original settlers of the village), and as a consequence, they feel that their social status is higher than that of newcomers. Moreover, while they will admit that Kafr el-Elow is located in the *Kism* of Helwan and that it thereby falls under the administrative jurisdiction of Helwan, they refuse to give their address as Kafr el-Elow-Helwan, unlike the majority of the younger natives and newcomers. In other words, old-timers still insist that Kafr el-Elow is a separate and distinct social community, while the younger generation and newcomers tend to view the village as a suburb of Helwan and to identify more strongly with this relatively large urban center than with Kafr el-Elow. That a strong sense of social solidarity and village pride is still prevalent even among the younger natives, however, is expressed by their disapproval of male newcomers who walk around the village after work to flirt with females.

In Chapter 4, I attempted to describe the religious institution in the village of Kafr el-Elow and to demonstrate its influence on the villagers' behavior. While every villager whom I encountered professed Islam as his religious faith, answers to my questions regarding daily prayer and the observance of the month of Ramadan made it apparent that significant modifications in religious practices had been made, especially by the younger generation. For example, only a minority of the younger generation said that they prayed daily and fasted during the month of Ramadan, although both practices are obligatory for all Muslims. Another religious modification which I observed was declining participation by native villagers in the *zar* cult rituals; most devotees are now women from outside the village. The use of charms for the prevention of illness and protection against the evil eye is, however, still widely practiced by the villagers of Kafr el-Elow. Modifications in religious practices might conceivably be attributed to the replacement of religious teaching by public education in the village, but despite the secularization process, Islam still plays a major role in Kafr el-Elow and in Egyptian society as a whole.

The increasing importance of formal education in Kafr el-Elow has had the effect of generating a new spirit of competition between families in the village. Parents frequently refer with pride to the fact that their sons are attending school, will soon be graduating, or are going to college, for a student's educational attainments reflect favorably on his entire extended family. In a sense, one person's attainments are regarded as those of his clan, enhancing its status in community. This phenomenon prevails not only in Kafr el-Elow, but throughout the Arab world. Indeed, due to the rising educational level of the male population in the village, the number of educated men in an extended family or clan is becoming as important a status criterion in Kafr el-Elow as was the size of the clan in the past. Educated members of an extended family help their kin by representing them in government matters, by assisting them in securing jobs, and by extricating them from trouble.

The trend toward more formal education in Kafr el-Elow has also produced significant changes in recreational activities. The young people of the village have built an athletic club with their own labor and at their own expense, despite the opposition of their parents, and have organized junior and senior soccer teams which compete with other teams from neighboring areas. The athletic club has fostered and strengthened the attachment of these young people to their community, for it is really the only facility in the village that prevents many young people from going to large urban centers such as Cairo or Helwan to spend their leisure time.

The mass media, especially the radio, have expanded the older as well as the younger villagers' horizons beyond their village community. Both the Suez crisis of 1956–1957 and the continuing Arab-Israeli conflict have induced many villagers to develop the habit of listening regularly to the news and the political speeches on their transistor radios. The transistor radio, which has been referred to as the most revolutionary invention in this age of mass communications, can be seen everywhere in the village: factory workers carry them in their hands on their way to and from their jobs, agricultural workers wear them on belts around their waists as they till their fields, and most shops and vendors' stands have them playing for the entertainment of their customers. The radio is such a tremendously effective social force in the village because it hurdles the illiteracy barrier. As one elderly man in the village expressed it: "Although I can't read, I am still informed, thanks to my transistor radio." For many villagers, therefore, this instrument is performing the function of a private tutor. The radio has also become a major tool of propaganda in the United Arab Republic, not only for political purposes, but also for promoting such social reform programs as family planning, which the government is trying desperately to implement. Finally, many villagers have been introduced to the urban way of life, especially in regard to consumption patterns, by the commercial advertisements that they hear on the radio. As the educational level of the villagers continues to rise, newspaper circulation will also undoubtedly become more widespread, producing other important changes in the attitudes, values, and behavior of Kafr el-Elow's residents.

Politically speaking, the villagers of Kafr el-Elow have assumed a new identity. After seventeen years of social and economic reform, the villagers are coming closer and closer to full participation in the political arena, from which all but the wealthy were excluded in the past. Even those who cannot read and write have broadened their vocabulary to include such political terms as imperialism, nationalism, freedom, socialism, election, and political responsibility. While most villagers do not fully understand the philosophical implications of such political terminology, the mere fact that they use it reflects a new trend; namely, an increased political awareness among the *fellaheen*.

An important factor which contributed to this new trend in Kafr el-Elow was the abolition of the traditional village government headed by the *omda*, who was not only the link and mediator between the village community and the central government in Cairo, but also the person who was responsible for the maintenance of stability and order in the village. The village acquired a new political status in 1960, when it became directly linked to the central government in Cairo through the subadministrative center in Helwan, and when the role of the new central government representative in the village—the *shaik il-balad*—was restricted to exclude responsibility for the resolution of disputes. As a further, unfortunate consequence of the latter, many villagers regard the *shaik* as a snob from an urban area who is not as interested in their welfare as was the traditional *omda*. They resent having to report their disputes to the newly-established police station in the village and having to go to Helwan or Cairo to take care of their own business affairs, matters which the *omda* formerly included among his services to the villagers. As the villagers come into more frequent contact with government officials, however, they will inevitably come more personally involved in their nation's political system.

Many significant economic changes have also occurred in Kafr el-Elow due to its rising per capita income, a trend which began when an increasing number of natives decided to leave farming and enter industrial employment or to engage in both occupations simultaneously, and which has been augmented by the influx of migrants, all of whom work in the factories surrounding the village. Even natives engaged exclusively in agriculture have shared in Kafr el-Elow's economic prosperity by shifting their production from annual to cash crops in order to meet the greater demand for foodstuffs resulting from an increasing population and changing food tastes. The majority of those engaged in agriculture are older persons and those who, for reasons other than advanced age, cannot secure factory jobs. Even extra field hands must usually be hired from outside the village: a situation in marked contrast with that prevailing in the past when there was always a surplus of labor in Kafr el-Elow. This shortage of agricultural workers also reflects the impact of industrialization on kinship ties in the village. In one family which I visited, the parents referred to their two sons who were working in the textile factory as *khawajat*, a term meaning "alien" or "foreigner," because they refused to help their father in the fields. This tendency is common among young people in the village of Kafr el-Elow and in Arab countries in general, indicating that they look down on agricultural work as degrading.

Rising per capita income in Kafr el-Elow may be attributed not only to industrial employment and marked changes in the quantity and quality of food consumption, but also to the demand for a greater variety of consumer goods and services in general. As a result, many villagers have invested their surplus incomes —their savings—in new businesses or in housing for rental purposes, as can be seen in the tremendous increase in the number of shops and occupations and the gradual conversion of agricultural land to residential use between 1940 and 1960. Other villagers have invested their savings in the renovation and improvement of their own homes, adding rooms and introducing such modern features as indoor plumbing and electricity. All these factors have combined to produce significant changes in the social class structure of the village, creating new criteria for personal evaluation and social placement.

In addition to stimulating the economy and diversifying the social class structure of Kafr el-Elow, the influx of migrants has promoted the introduction of post office service and the provision of more frequent bus transportation in the village. Prior to the late 1950s, there was very little demand for bus service because few people left the village to visit friends and relatives or to work in industry; those who did the former were gone only a few days, and business was transacted almost exclusively within the village. Whatever mail traffic took place was conducted through the *omda*'s home. Since that time, however, these conditions no longer prevail in Kafr el-Elow: postal service has become the daily routine of a government agent appointed for this purpose by the central government in Cairo, and bus transportation to Helwan or Cairo is available every 20 minutes throughout the day and more frequently at peak demand periods.

## Change in Kafr el-Elow

The changes which have taken place during the last four decades in the village of Kafr el-Elow have spread from the urban center, Cairo, to this peasant community. As is generally characteristic of cultural diffusion, innovations of a material nature were first introduced, and they, in turn, produced alterations in the traditional attitudes and values of the community. Therefore, this analysis of the total process of social change in the village will begin with a cursory review of the material culture changes that have taken place in Kafr el-Elow since 1930.

As was noted earlier, Kafr el-Elow was a relatively stable agricultural community during the early 1920s because the rate of change was not sufficiently rapid to produce any social disorganization. The slowness of change not only reflected the community's physical isolation from urban areas, due to the lack of communication facilities and the absence of paved roads, but also the prevalence of illiteracy among the inhabitants of the village. With the establishment of a cement factory, the installation of a water pump for irrigation, and the advent of a modern transportation system during the third decade of this century, the process of modernization was initiated in the village. While these early material culture innovations did not immediately affect the majority of the villagers, they at least created a new awareness of modern technology in the community.

By 1966, impressive technological changes had taken place. For example, with the rapid increase of industrial employment and the concomitant need to get to work at a specific time, wristwatches had become very common among the villagers. More than 200 watches had been sold by one of the village school teachers alone; other villagers had secured theirs from outside Kafr el-Elow. Bicycles were being used by some villagers to travel to and from work, and youngsters were renting bicycles for pleasure rides around the village. Transistor radios had become a widespread means of communication, having an especially dramatic impact upon the lives of the illiterate segment of the population. Whereas prior to 1945 no radios existed in Kafr el-Elow, by 1966 villagers had purchased over 500 transistor radios from one of the village school teachers alone, and six villagers even owned television sets. Electricity, which had been introduced into Kafr el-Elow in 1960, was being used for illumination and other power needs in private homes as well as in public facilities. Butane gas stoves, canned foods, and items like soft drinks, beer, and cigarettes had also become increasingly common in Kafr el-Elow's homes, reflecting the higher standard of living expected by the village population. These rising expectations, in combination with the continually increasing village population due to industrialization, had resulted in a tremendous expansion of commercial units in Kafr el-Elow: from six businesses in 1930 to seventy-eight in 1966, many of them offering goods and services which were unavailable in the village prior to 1960. Population growth had also been responsible for the tremendous expansion of housing facilities in Kafr el-Elow: many old homes were remodeled and enlarged, and new single residences and apartments had been constructed for rental purposes.

Teachers, who had increased in number from one to sixteen since secular education was introduced in 1933, also constitued important agents of social change in Kafr el-Elow, not only by accelerating the literacy rate, but also in terms of influencing the values and attitudes of the villagers, because teachers, as such, are very highly regarded in Kafr el-Elow as they are throughout the Middle East. Most impressive was the new trend among village youths to pursue higher education; for the first time in Kafr el-Elow's history, sons of villagers were graduating from institutions of higher learning in Cairo and in other urban areas. While the increasing importance of formal education in Kafr el-Elow was directly reflected, as has been mentioned, in larger school enrollments, an increase in the number of teachers, and in higher educational aspirations, it was more indirectly expressed in the higher income level of the villagers, resulting, in part, from their ability to engage in better-paying occupations than the traditional one of farming: occupations demanding specialized training and skills. As the new technology had expanded with the introduction, since the 1930s, of more machines and tools into the village, occupational opportunities characteristic of urban centers had become increasingly available.

It should seem quite clear from the preceding discussion that many changes which occurred during this thirty-six-year period between 1930 and 1966 have significantly altered the character of the village, so that the most advanced forms of modern industry coexist today with age-old methods of subsistence cultivation, and a modern urban community is arising in the midst of folk groups. Interestingly enough, Redfield and Lewis used this same technique—namely, tracing a community's history through three decades—to study social change in Tepoztlan, Mexico (Redfield 1964; Lewis 1960). Two questions which Redfield and Lewis (and others) have raised about the influence of industrialization upon folk societies are relevant to this study; namely:

1. What are the implications of industrialization and urbanization for kinship organization in the village?
2. What are the implications of industrialization and urbanization for social stratification in the village?

While sufficient time has not yet elapsed since the advent of large-scale industrialization in Kafr el-Elow (1952) to enable me to answer such questions fully, a few comparisons can be made between some general anthropological remarks and changes I observed during my two-year stay in the village.

During the past fifteen years, the long-established principle that industrialization and urbanization break down kinship organization has been questioned by several noted anthropologists. Raymond Firth has reformulated the theory of the relation of industrialization to family organization in terms of recent historical and sociological research.

> What the development towards an industrial society probably does is to break down the *formal structure* of kin groups, except perhaps that of the elementary family, which is most resistant. The lineage, the extended family, the large cooperative, cognatic kin unit is likely not to survive as its members disperse into industrial employment and their traditional resources and authority structures lose meaning. But *personal kin ties* tend to be strengthened if the physical isolation of the elementary family is promoted by industrial, urban conditions. There is no reason then to think that extra-familial kin ties are likely to decrease in our Western society. (Firth 1964, 83)

Similarly, Singer, attempting to gain deeper insight into the functional relation between industrialization, urbanization, and modernization, and the Indian joint family, came to the following conclusion:

> In a preliminary . . . study of a group of outstandingly successful industrial leaders in Madras City, I found that, while there have been striking changes within three generations in residential, occupational, educational and social mobility, as well as in patterns of ritual observances, these changes have not transformed the traditional joint family structure into isolated nuclear families. On the contrary, the urban and industrial members of the family maintain numerous ties and obligations with members of the family who have remained in the ancestral village or town or have moved elsewhere. And within the urban and industrial setting a modified joint family organization is emerging. The metropolitan industrial center has simply become a new arena for the working of the joint family system.
>
> It is not at all true that the joint family system is structurally and functionally incompatible with modern industry and is, therefore, either a major obstacle to the development of industry or is inevitably destroyed by the progress of industry. (Singer 1968:444–445)

My observations in Kafr el-Elow coincide with Firth's and Singer's findings, even though my families did not have to move away from their village setting in order to experience the industrialization process, as was done in the case of Singer's families. Of course, one might readily conclude that if the extended family does not break down under the impact of industrialization when this involves moving from a village to a large city, there would be less of a tendency for it to do so when no change of locale occurs. Although an overall breakdown did not occur, I nevertheless observed two *adaptations to industrialization* among Kafr el-Elow's extended families; namely, compartmentalization and vicarious ritualization. These two processes were also employed by Singer's industrial leaders' families to maintain or modify joint family structure in the urban-industrial setting of Madras.

Compartmentalization, in Kafr el-Elow as in Madras, means that behavior approved at the office or factory is quite different from that considered appropriate at home (Singer 1968:438). As was indicated in the discussion of village economy, industrial workers may wear Western-style clothing and employ modern science and technology at work, but upon returning home each evening, they revert to their traditional style of life. Vicarious ritualization, the second adaptive technique employed to reduce the conflict between the traditional and modern spheres of life, means that young men who spend eight to ten hours a day working at a factory and traveling to and from their jobs, and who cannot, therefore, devote as much time to observing various religious rituals as did their fathers or grandfathers, may, for example, contract their daily prayers from several hours to several minutes (Singer 1968:439).

Answers to a structured questionnaire revealed that only 26 percent of the younger respondents in Kafr el-Elow prayed daily, the remaining 74 percent praying less regularly. By contrast, older respondents replied almost unanimously that they prayed daily. Similarly, the majority of the younger respondents reported that they did not fast regularly during the month of Ramadan. These tendencies, however, do not imply that the younger generation is abandoning or turning against religion. While insisting upon their allegiance to Islam, they maintain that some modification in religious practices is necessitated by changes in other aspects of their lives. Weddings, birth ceremonies, and other life-cycle rites have also been contracted or consolidated by extended families to accommodate their members who are employed by industry. For example, the mourning period following a funeral, which formerly lasted forty days in Kafr el-Elow, now never exceeds one week in length. In other words, vicarious ritualization is one of the major ways in which industrial workers and their families may "modernize" their lives, adapting to industrial conditions without abandoning tradition. These data seem to suggest that the *aila* (joint family) in Kafr el-Elow may undergo a change of organization without losing its essential character. Despite the fact that some villagers have left their joint family households to establish their own nuclear families in separate residential units, their families continue to subscribe to the norms of the joint family system and do not abandon their joint family obligations.

Social stratification is the second aspect of life in Kafr el-Elow which should be re-examined. According to Redfield, personal biographies provide significant insights into the phenomenon of social mobility in a community.

> The respect in which a community is not one stable and self-consistent structure, but changes from one manner of life to another, appears most plainly in the changing states of mind of people, or in the differences between what older people think and feel and what younger people think and feel. We might, therefore, attempt a comparison of the careers of older and younger people by obtaining the life stories of representatives of each generation. (Redfield 1961:60)

The case histories of families living in Kafr el-Elow reflect a definite upgrading in occupational status over a period of several generations. And when census data were checked to establish the validity of this case history information, a clearcut trend of occupational mobility manifested itself. In 1960 the relative incidence of the two categories of employment in Kafr el-Elow—agriculture and industry (which includes mining)—was a complete reversal of the situation that prevailed in 1937. Whereas agriculture claimed 76 percent of all villagers engaged in some occupation in 1937, it claimed only 27 percent in 1960, in spite of the fact that the amount of acreage under cultivation had doubled during the twenty-three year period. On the other other hand, there was a 300 percent increase in the number of villagers engaged in industry over the span of a generation, and an even greater rate of increase may be expected in the future. It may be safely stated, therefore, that the village occupational structure has changed from one that is essentially agricultural to one that is based primarily on industrial employment. This trend has naturally resulted in a marked increase in the number of professional and skilled workers among villagers in Kafr el-Elow, most of whom are found among the younger generation.

Consequently, I conclude that the relatively unstratified village population will be gradually replaced by a class-structured community in which status and social mobility are based on personal achievement. As per capita income continues to rise, competition or rivalry among the villagers will undoubtedly become more intense, portending a truly dynamic community. The less intimate relations resulting from this trend were already becoming obvious when I was in the village.

Many times, when taking pictures of various sites, I was stopped and questioned about my purposes by newcomers, even though I was always accompanied on these occasions by a school teacher who was the son of a prominent leader in Kafr el-Elow. Most of them did not recognize the teacher and he, in turn, did not recognize most of them. I predict, moreover, that the majority of Kafr el-Elow's population will eventually become an urban proletariat, agricultural employment disappearing with the complete transfer of land use from farming to residential purposes in order to accommodate the ever-increasing flow of workers migrating to the village in search of employment in the surrounding industrial complex. The village of Kafr el-Elow, therefore, constitutes prototype of a community evolving from a relatively classless, agricultural, folk society to a stratified, industrial, modern society, a prototype which may be predictive not only of future trends in Egyptian society, but also of what will happen to traditional communities in other societies under the influence of industrialization.

# 8

# Kafr el-Elow Revisited

## An Analysis of Continuity and Discontinuity of Change

*The second phase of this research project was carried out in Kafr el-Elow between December 1985 and July 1986 under the terms of a Fulbright research fellowship, and a research grant from the American Research Center in Egypt and the University of Michigan-Flint.*

*During that period, I was affiliated with the Social Research Center at the American University in Cairo. To Dr. Laila Shukry el-Hamamsy, the Director, I am grateful for her support. I owe a great deal to my colleague and field assistant Mr. Muhammad Fikri and all of those who participated in collecting the information needed for this project.*

*Finally, I would like once again to thank the people of Kafr el-Elow for their cooperation, courtesy and hospitality.*

The main objective of this chapter is to re-examine and analyze the change which has been occurring in Kafr el-Elow during the past two decades (1966-1986). When the first phase of this research came to an end in 1966, a very definite struggle for dominance was being waged between the new industrial-urban order and the traditional peasant-agricultural order. Though many changes were still in operation, their effects had not yet become significant.

Since 1966, the investigator has maintained contact with the people in Kafr el-Elow by visiting the community on a regular basis at least once every two years. In December 1985, the investigator returned to Kafr el-Elow to re-examine and analyze the same community as it exists during the mid-1980's, giving special attention to changes that occurred during the previous twenty years.

In 1966, Kafr el-Elow was incorporated into the adjacent city of Helwan, the administrative center for the southern part of the Cairo governorate, and was thereby officially re-zoned an urban area. It constitutes one of ten *shiyakhat* (police precincts) which constitute the local council for *qism* Helwan (division), the southern administrative part for the Cairo governorate. It is, therefore, imperative to view Kafr el-Elow as part of the larger society, because it is fully incorporated politically, economically, and socially with the Cairo governorate. Since Kafr el-Elow also has been affected by many national events, the following analysis will examine these and consider their impact at the national and local levels.

## The National Scene: Egypt

During the past two decades (1966-1986), Egypt experienced great changes demographically, economically, politically, and socially. Their impact and ramifications have been felt at all socio-economic levels. Several major forces have contributed to the process and the direction of change.

I. Rapid population growth constitutes a critical factor in the changing socio-economic characteristics of Egypt. Egypt's population has increased by at least 20 million people during the past two decades, from 30.1 million in 1966 to over 50 million in 1986. Population increased at an average rate of 2.4 percent a year from 1966 to 1976 and 2.7 percent a year during 1976-1986. The main factors which contributed to this steady growth are a high birthrate and a decline in the crude death rate (see Table I).

TABLE I
NATALITY, MORTALITY, AND NATURAL POPULATION INCREASE*

| Year | Crude Birth Rate per Thousand | Crude Death Rate per Thousand | Natural Rate of Increase per Thousand |
|------|------|------|------|
| 1952 | 45.2 | 17.8 | 27.4 |
| 1960 | 42.9 | 16.9 | 26.0 |
| 1966 | 40.9 | 15.8 | 25.1 |
| 1970 | 35.1 | 15.1 | 20.0 |
| 1973 | 35.8 | 13.0 | 22.8 |
| 1976 | 36.6 | 11.8 | 24.8 |
| 1980 | 37.5 | 10.0 | 27.5 |
| 1983 | 37.6 | 10.0 | 27.6 |
| 1984 | 38.4 | 9.4 | 29.0 |

*Source: *Egypt Statistical Yearbook, 1952-1985* (Cairo, Egypt: 1986).

The crude death rate steadily declined from 16.9 per 1000 in the early 1960's to 11.8 per 1000 during the 1970's and 9.4 per 1000 in 1984. Furthermore, improved public health measures have halved the death rate for children ages 1-4, from 34 per 1000 in the early 1960's to 16 per 1000 in the early 1980's. Between 1966 and the mid-1980's, life expectancies rose from 51.6 to 55.9 for males and from 53.8 to 58.4 for females.

Egypt's population growth has been accompanied by fast urban expansion due to the influx of peasants from villages to urban centers in general and to the Cairo governorate in particular (see Table II).

TABLE II
DENSITY AND RATE OF POPULATION GROWTH
FOR THE CAIRO GOVERNORATE (1966-1985)*

| Years | 1966 | 1976 | 1985 |
|---|---|---|---|
| Cairo population | 4,230,000 | 5,084,000 | 6,208,000 |
| % of total population | 14.0 | 13.3 | 12.7 |
| Density/sq km | 19,594 | 23,737 | 28,506 |

*Source: Egypt Statistical Yearbook, 1952-1985. Cairo, Egypt: 1986).

The population of the Cairo governorate has increased by nearly 50 percent during the past two decades. In 1985, the greater Cairo metropolitan area's population has been estimated at more than ten million people, or nearly 20.7 percent of Egypt's total population. The impact of population growth has had economic and social implications not only for urban centers, but also for the society at large. Population growth is considered as the most serious problem facing Egypt. Nearly half of Egypt's population consists of young people, 17 years of age and under, who must be fed, housed, clothed, and educated. It has been estimated that nearly 20 percent of the children who reach school age (six years) are not admitted to school because of the shortage of classroom space. The impact of population growth is also felt in the demand for housing.

In an interview with the Al-Ahram on November 13, 1981, Mr. Kafrawi, the Minister of Housing and Reconstruction, pointed out that "Egypt's housing needs will exceed 3,600,000 units by the year 2000." He emphasized that "the government needs to spend L.E 20 billion (Egyptian pounds), or at the rate of L.E one billion per year for the next 20 years just to meet Egypt's basic housing needs."

The housing crisis and the high population density are visible everywhere in Egypt. These twin problems have created a difficult dilemma, especially for urban governorates in Egypt, and an impact on the social, economic, and environmental levels as reflected in Table II.

Since 1965, the Egyptian government has formally recognized population growth as a major national problem. A family planning and birth control program was initiated nationwide by the government, despite the total opposition from Islamic fundamentalist groups. The formal government policy of family planning and birth control has been ineffective in curbing the nation's population growth, especially among the rural population and low income urban dwellers whose religious and cultural values remain hostile to such policy.

II. The inability of the agricultural sector to keep pace with increasing population has resulted in a steady increase in food imports since the mid-1960's.

By 1974, Egypt had become a net importer of agricultural commodities for the first time in its history. This trend has continued; as of 1984-1985, more than seven million metric tons of wheat, maize, and other varieties of food were imported.[1] Most of the imported food is sold to the public at 50-70 percent below cost in order to keep it within the reach of low income groups. The cost of food subsidy has been growing steadily from a few million L.E during the mid-1960's to more than L.E 2 billion by the mid-1980's.

Traditionally, agriculture was the largest and most dominant sector in the national economy; however, the stagnation of agriculture which began in the late 1960's has continued through the early 1980's, growing at an average rate of two percent per year. This low rate of agricultural growth is not sufficient to keep pace with the rate of population growth.

In addition to population growth, other factors contributed to the decline in agricultural productivity. Two of these factors were the decrease in economic investment in agriculture and the influx of peasants from rural to urban areas in Egypt and to the oil producing countries of the Middle East. This migration led to a shortage of agricultural workers in rural Egypt. Furthermore, more than one million acres of good agricultural land has been taken out of cultivation as a result of urban expansion. This figure amounts to nearly 17-20 percent of Egypt's good arable lands. The fragmentation of agricultural land and government agricultural policy have also contributed to a low productivity rate.[2]

III. The Arab-Israeli War influenced Egypt's social and economic direction. The 1967 war with Israel forced Egypt to abandon its ambitious economic plan which formerly had proved successful. During the first half of the 1960's, Egypt's economy grew at an average rate of 6 percent a year; however, Egypt's defense burden added to its continuous increase of foreign debts which was estimated by the world bank at $17 billion in 1980 and $36 billion in 1986.[3] Egypt's peace treaty with Israel in the mid-1970's led to some changes in the direction and planning of the nation's economy.

IV. Dramatic national political changes influenced socio-economic development during the 1960's and the 1970's. First, Egypt experienced dramatic domestic changes during President Nasser's era. As is illustrated in the first phase of this study, the Nasser government built an impressive dominant public sector of the economy. During that period, some valuable national economic developments were accomplished in areas such as the iron, steel, and other heavy industries. Egypt's industrial development grew at an average rate of 6 percent between 1960-1965. Furthermore, Nasser's government initiated its socialistic economic program, which led to the nationalization of Egypt's major means of production and distribution, as well as its financial institutions. Nasser's socialist policies led to the decrease of the private sector's role in Egypt's

---

[1]For further information see: *World Bank, World Development Report, 1985* (New York: Oxford University Press, 1985).

[2]For further information see: *Al-Ahram Iktisadi, No. 764* (1983) [in Arabic].

[3]Jabber, Paul, "Egypt's Crisis, America's Dilemma," *Foreign Affairs*, 64:960-80, (Summer 1986).

economy. At the same time, the public sector emerged to play the dominant role and shape the direction of Egypt's economic development. During this period, the new government policy gave the working class more protection and benefits than ever before in the history of modern Egypt.

Nasser's socialist reforms yielded some success during the initial stage. After the 1967 war, however, the rate of economic growth started declining and economic stagnation prevailed. Several factors contributed to the decline of economic growth: the impact of the 1967 Arab-Israeli war, the defense burden, the lack of available funds for economic development, and poor management. In addition, an outdated and entrenched bureaucracy paralyzed thinking and initiative.

After the death of Mr. Nasser in September 1970 and the succession of Mr. Sadat to the presidency, Egypt experienced another drastic economic change. The poor performance of the economic public sector was used by the Sadat regime as a justification to restructure Egypt's economy. The centralized economic policy developed during the 1960's by the Nasser regime was dismantled and replaced by *al-in fitah al-iqtisadi* (the open-door economic policy). In order to create a suitable climate for foreign capital investment in Egypt, the People's Assembly passed Law 43 on June 9, 1974, clearly giving assurances and protection to investors. The new open-door policy was to revitalize Egypt's economy not only by granting protection to foreign investors, but also by giving customs and tax concessions. Despite the publicity in the Egyptian press, the economic pay-off from the open-door policy has not been impressive. Luxury goods such as cars, clothes by European designers, home appliances, cosmetics, and other items flood the Egyptian market and are available only for those who have the means. The open-door economic policy initiated by the Sadat regime not only had a disastrous effect on consumer expenditure, but also widened the gap between the haves and have-nots in Egypt.[4] President Sadat's open-door economic policy benefited a small but powerful group due to the widespread corruption which is one of the legacies of the Sadat era. Furthermore, the new economic policy contributed to political instability and encouraged the rise of Egypt's militant Moslem fundamentalist movement.

V. The fifth event which contributed to a significant change in Egypt's socio-economic structure was the increase of oil prices which resulted from the 1973 Arab-Israeli War. The influx of oil revenue into the oil producing countries of the Persian Gulf area created an economic bonanza. The economic boom generated a great deal of employment in the gulf area and opened the door for millions of foreign workers.

Egyptian citizens flocked to the oil producing countries in large numbers to fill professional and non-professional positions, skilled and non-skilled jobs. The number of Egyptians working outside Egypt as of 1984 has been estimated at 3.5-4 million according to government officials. Their earning power has

[4]For further information on Sadat's economic policy see: Hamied Ansari, *Egypt, the Stalled Society* (New York: State University of New York Press, 1986). Also, B. Hansen and S. Radwan, *Al-amal wa il adle il-ijtimaii fi masr il-thamanenat* (Cairo: Dar il-Mustaqbil il-arabi Press, 1983). [in Arabic].

been estimated at $8-9 billion a year; however, the remittances by Egyptians working in oil producing countries during the previous decade have fluctuated and have been estimated at $1-4 billion a year.[5] The infusion of such large sums of foreign currency into the Egyptian economy influenced its direction and had an impact visible in all aspects of the society.

The following analysis reveals the changing trends and the rise of new social and economic characteristics within Egypt.

A. In the beginning, notably during the later part of the 1950's and the 1960's, migration was internal, an influx from rural to urban areas, especially to Cairo and Alexandria. Since the early 1970's, this trend started changing at a very rapid rate; people moved from both the rural and urban areas of Egypt to other oil producing countries of the Persian Gulf and North Africa. Significant changes occurred in people's views, values, and outlooks. Traditionally, Egyptians in general had not been eager to leave their homes to travel into other countries. The numbers of those who travelled were small and limited to the elite and well-to-do within the society. Furthermore, even internal traveling from various villages to urban areas like Cairo and Alexandria was limited to a very small percentage of that segment of the Egyptian population.

The new trend, therefore, reflects drastic changes in the way people think and define their new roles and expectations both socially and economically. It is not unusual to hear that at least one member of each household is working outside Egypt. The number of those working could even be larger, if restrictions on traveling by the host countries were lifted. Many of those who were unable to obtain a visa from the oil producing countries went to non-oil producing ones like Jordan and Yemen in search of a job to improve their economic condition.

B. The impact of the oil economy and the new mobility led not only to the improvement of the economic condition of millions of Egyptians, but contributed to a change in their consumption pattern and also created new social expectations. This consumption pattern is reflected in the new demand for various consumer goods such as home appliances, different varieties of food, clothing, and even types of entertainment. The availability of such consumer goods in the market, however, was not enough to satisfy increasing demands. As a result, a shortage of goods contributed to a continuous increase in prices. At the same time, it triggered a new rate of inflation which fluctuated from 15-30 percent a year during the past decade (1975-1985). This situation also was stimulated by the open-door economic policy. Professor Ibrahim referred to this trend by stating that:

> Not counting what Egyptians abroad bring with them, Egypt's imports of consumer goods have steadily grown from L.E 36 million in 1970 to L.E 133 million in 1975, to L.E 1,224 million in 1979 and are projected to reach L.E 1,331 million in 1980. In short, Egypt's imports of consumer goods in one decade have increased by 3,600 percent compared with only a 2,000 per-

[5]Egyptian Government, "Egyptian Workers Outside Egypt," Ministry of Labor and Manpower (Cairo: unpublished, 1985) [in Arabic].

cent increase in capital goods. Neither population growth nor the rate of inflation in one decade would justify this steep rise in the importation of consumer goods. The main factor that explains it is the real increase in levels of consumption, expecially luxury goods.[6]

The possession of material goods such as cars, home appliances (refrigerators, televisions, video recorders, cooking ranges, washing machines, and other electrical gadgets) is an important social and economic indicator which reflects success and, at the same time, enhances the individual's status among his relatives and friends.

C. The new mobility trends, especially in the rural sector of the Egyptian society, created a shortage of agricultural workers in many villages. This situation caused an increase in farm workers' wages which, in the mid-1980's, are averaging between L.E 6 to L.E 8 per day,[7] compared to L.E 1/2 per day during the 1960's. Furthermore, the new situation altered the peasants' working habits. The traditional working day in the agricultural field started with sunrise and ended with sunset. At the present, eight hours is the average working day for a hired agricultural worker. This situation, among other factors, contributed to a decline in workers' agricultural productivity and turned most Egyptian villages from food producing into consuming units.

VI. During the previous two decades, as a result of the 1952 revolution, drastic changes took place in higher education. Traditionally, higher education was limited in general to the privileged class. This situation started changing slowly during the 1950's and began to accelerate during the 1960's and 1970's. Student enrollments were expanded significantly at the traditional academic institutions, such as Cairo University, Ainshams University, Al-Azhar University and the University of Alexandria. In addition many new universities were established all over Egypt, such as El-Mania University, El-Munifia University, El-Zagazig University, Aswan University, Tanta University, Helwan University and Suez-Canal University. These academic institutions opened their doors to all of those who were qualified to enroll without regard to their socio-economic background. Education was and still is free-of-charge to students.

This educational policy opened a new avenue for the offspring of many of the underprivileged class who were at the bottom of the socio-economic scale. This access to a college education facilitated their upward social mobility. Many of those who graduated from universities began to occupy important positions in both the private and the public sector of the Egyptian society. Such positions traditionally had been reserved for the privileged class. During the academic year 1982-1983, more than 100,000 students graduated from colleges and other higher academic institutions (Al-Ahram Iktisadi: No. 799, 1984). The

---

[6] Saad Eddin Ibrahim, *The New Arab Social Order: A Study of the Impact of Oil Wealth* (Boulder: Westview Press, 1982), p. 89.

[7] Although farm workers are paid L.E 6-8 per day, more than twice what the average civil servant earns, the exodus of farm laborers to Iraq, Jordan, and the Persian Gulf countries and the disdain that young people have for farming have produced a severe labor shortage in agriculture.

increasing number of university graduates contributed to an alteration of Egypt's social structure. Despite the increase in the number of college graduates, the Egyptian economy has failed to expand fast enough to create more jobs for those who need them. The civil service has been the main agency which absorbed hundreds of thousands of university graduates. Their appointments reflect political rather than economic rationales. The newly appointed graduate's monthly earnings are very meager balanced against the high cost of living. For example, a new college graduate appointee will earn L.E 45 per month[8] (or the equivalent of nearly $35).

Although there has been an increase in the national wealth, its uneven distribution has made the disparity between the incomes of the rich and poor more striking than ever before. Those affected the most are government employees, whose numbers were estimated in 1986 at around 3.5 million. Despite some rise in the standard of living, nearly half of the Egyptian population are ill-fed and ill-housed.[9]

## The Local Scene: Kafr el-Elow

How has Kafr el-Elow changed in the light of these national events? And how has Kafr el-Elow altered as a result of the changes which took place in the immediate vicinity and adjacent to its boundaries?

### The Setting

Kafr el-Elow and its surrounding area has changed greatly. The main route of travel to the community is a newly constructed four-lane highway divided by a narrow traffic island. On the approach from Cairo, extending along both sides of the highway and into the Marazeek Bridge is a maze of industrial and commercial outlets. Most common establishments lining the highway are mechanical repair shops and other service outlets for trucks and small cars, carpentry and electrical shops, and other small manufacturing firms such as those producing spaghetti and pasta, ice cream cones, and ceramic or bathroom equipment. Other kinds of heavy and light industries are also located nearby such as petro-chemical, electrical, home manufacturing, paper, iron and steel industries.

The newly built highway, when completed, will further facilitate transportation between upper and lower Egypt and will increase traffic density, which already has a negative effect on the surrounding physical environment.

In addition to the newly constructed highway, a new metro line was built through the eastern side of the community. Passing through Kafr el-Elow, Helwan, and Cairo, the new transportation line links the industrial area in the southern part of the Cairo governorate with its northern section. It is known as the Cairo-Helwan Metro Line, which is part of the new extension of the

[8]One dollar is the equivalent of L.E 1.3 according to the official rate as of 1986.

[9]For further information on poverty, see: Unni Wikam, *Among the Poor in Cairo* (USA: Tamstack Publications, 1980). Also, Amr Mohie El-din, "Income Distribution and Basic Needs in Urban Egypt," *Cairo Papers in Social Science*, Vol. 5 (November 1982). [Cairo: American University in Cairo Press).

*The new highway, which is built through the old agricultural fields.*

*The old main road.*

underground and aboveground transportation system within the greater Cairo metropolitan area. This newly built metro line will be completed in 1987. It is expected to carry 60,000 passengers per hour during peak traffic time. Not only will it facilitate the movement of a large segment of the work force in the area, but it will also have an impact on the physical and economic conditions of Kafr el-Elow. In addition to the construction of the new highway and the metro line, several new streets were built inside the community as a result of the physical growth which took place during the last two decades.

The physical expansion within and near the community's boundaries during the past two decades has ruined the old ecological setting of Kafr el-Elow. The green vegetation which stretched from the west side of the community to the banks of the Nile River and gave Kafr el-Elow its physical rural characteristics has disappeared. In addition, the air pollution in the area has already reached a dangerous level, threatening the lives of the population in the area. Between 1981 and 1984, the government office for industrialization (GOFI) in co-operation with Cairo University, the National Academy of Science and Technology, and an American consulting group (Weston International, Inc.) conducted a lengthy survey of the quality of air and water resources in Egypt. The survey reveals that air and water pollution has reached a dangerous level, especially around certain industrial zones. The report points out that the Nile River is polluted throughout its length in Egypt. This pollution comes from industrial plants, the majority of which are owned and managed by the government. The report also reveals that the air also suffers greatly from industry. In Kafr el-Elow and the adjacent area of Helwan, the pollution has already reached a dangerous level from the cement dust emissions and other industrial pollutant sources such as the iron, steel, chemical, and petrol gas industries in that area. The GOFI report further reveals that the cement factories alone pump 293 tons of dust into the atmosphere daily; 195 tons per square mile fall daily to the ground. Furthermore, the cement dust in the atmosphere is enough to kill almost all the trees in the area.[10]

This problem has been recognized by the government, and the mass media refer to it frequently, but, so far, not much has been done to remedy this dangerous situation.

## Population

From a demographic viewpoint, Kafr el-Elow's population has increased from around 6,700 people in 1966 to 14,495 in 1976, to an approximate population of nearly 30,000 people in 1986. Kafr el-Elow doubled its population

---

[10]Precise data on water quality in the Nile River is fragmented. However, the Water Pollution Laboratory of the National Research Center, the Nile River Committee, and the Academy of Science and Technology Research showed that the Nile River was polluted and support the finding of the GOFI report. The GOFI report is an unpublished government document in Arabic (1985). Also, fragmented reports were published by the mass media on industrial pollution. For further information see *Cairo Today*, Vol. 7 (January 1986). Also *akhir-saa*, May 15, 1985.

*Pre-fab housing factory.*

*Petro-Gas pumping station.*

once every ten years during the past two decades (1966-1986).[11] This rapid population growth exceeded the national rate. It is attributed to the high natural birthrate, in addition to the flow of migrant workers who came from different parts of Egypt to work in various industrial outlets in the area and settled in Kafr el-Elow. It has been estimated that nearly half of the community's population consists of migrant workers. Their demographic impact has changed Kafr el-Elow's traditional homogeneous character into a heterogeneous one. This impact is clear to the elderly population, but is not noticeable to the younger generation.

The annual rate of population growth in Kafr el-Elow is still higher than the national average as a whole: 3.0 percent versus 2.9 percent as of 1985. The high rate of population growth is attributed to the continuation of high birthrate and a steady decrease in the death rate. Furthermore, the improvement in health care, hygienic condition, and diet contributed to the decrease in the crude death rate, especially the infant mortality rate. This situation led to a larger family size in Kafr el-Elow, which consists of six people, compared to the national average, which consists of 5.6 people per family. Half of Kafr el-Elow's population is comprised of those 17 years of age and under, and, thus, is consistent with the national average.

From the preceding analysis, it is safe to indicate that the family planning and birth control program was neither effective nor successful in Kafr el-Elow. In a survey conducted among two hundred subjects in Kafr el-Elow in which the respondents were asked about their views of family planning and birth control, eighty-nine percent of the respondents said that they oppose birth control, because it is against Islamic beliefs. Many of the respondents expressed the belief that "children are the gift of God." Some others justified their total opposition to any family planning and birth control by reciting the following from the Koran:

> There is no moving creature on earth
> But its sustenance depends on Allah:
> He knoweth the time and place
> of its definite abode and its
> Temporary deposit:
> All is in a clear record book.
> (The Holy Koran-Surah 11, Verse 6)

> Kill not your children for fear of want: we shall provide
> sustenance for them as well as for you.
> (The Holy Koran-Surah 17, Verse 31)

The general views of people in Kafr el-Elow toward family planning and birth control tend to be consistent with the nation at large. Also, their views reflect the impact of the increased religiosity in Kafr el-Elow.

[11]All statistical data were collected from *Egypt Census Books,* 1966 and 1976 and *Egypt Statistical Year Book,* 1955-1985 (Cairo: 1986).

## Health

The health conditions of people in Kafr el-Elow show steady improvement. The decline in the infant mortality rate, the decrease in the crude death rate, and the expansion of life expectancy indicate an improvement in physical health conditions in general.

According to information provided by two physicians in the village and the public health nurse, who indicated that people now have better medical care than before, people now rely less on folk medicine and more on modern medicine for the treatment of their diseases. Also, they pointed out that there are fewer infectious diseases such as tuberculosis and typhoid. The vast majority of people have refrigeration, which reduces the possibility of food contamination, a factor which, in the past, used to contribute to infections and food poisoning.

The number of physicians has increased from one during the 1960's to ten during the 1980's. In addition, a free health care service is available at a mosque which is managed by an organized religious group in Kafr el-Elow. The availability of physicians in Kafr el-Elow encourages people to seek their help rather than having to go to Helwan or Cairo, which used to deter people. The general awareness of good health among the people of Kafr el-Elow has improved during the past two decades. The construction of a sewage system which is almost completed will further contribute to a better hygienic condition for the community.

## Housing and Physical Expansion

The increase in the size of population, among other factors, has also led to a vast expansion of old homes and the construction of new ones for personal use and as a commercial investment. Row upon row of multi-level new houses and commercial outlets are built. Nearly all of the construction which took place on both sides of the streets and of the highway consists of commercial outlets on the ground level and living units on the upper levels. The highest percentage of the construction consists of the multi-level type, which reflects typical urban characteristics. Most of the newly built homes contain running water and electricity. Some include new physical features which did not exist in the past, such as modern kitchens with many electrical appliances and western bathrooms. Such innovations change the style of living.

Another factor which contributed to the new style of housing with modern construction is the money paid in advance by the potential renters to the landlord. This money, referred to as *khelow* (key money), varies from L.E 1000 to L.E 5000. The key money will not be counted toward the rent nor toward the price of the unit if it is put up for sale. This money gives the donors priority over others. Despite the fact that key money is illegal, its occurrence prevails in the country as a whole. It is a common practice for some landlords who are unable to provide the financial cost of construction to rely heavily on the key money obtained in advance to complete the construction of their buildings. This practice is the result of a housing shortage not only in Kafr el-Elow, but nationwide.

*The new modern housing expansion on agricultural land.*

*Vertical housing expansion in the old site of Kafr el-Elow.*

Housing is a critical issue for the majority of people at all socio-economic levels. The pressing demand for land to build on in Kafr el-Elow contributed to a drastic increase in real estate prices during the past two decades. In the mid-1960's, the average price for one acre of land in the area was around L.E 900-L.E 1000. In the mid-1980's, the average price per one acre of land has reached around L.E 250,000. As a matter of fact, land for building is sold by the square meter now, and the prices vary from L.E 150/sq. meter to L.E 250/sq. meter. The price is determined by the location of the land. All of the new commercial and industrial expansion within and adjacent to Kafr el-Elow occurred on agricultural lands which traditionally used to be the main source of subsistence for the majority of the people in that community. As of the summer of 1986, nearly 90% of the land which had been under cultivation during the 1960's has been used for urban and industrial expansion.

Despite the high cost of construction, the housing expansion which took place in Kafr el-Elow has spurred the community's economy. Another factor which fueled this physical growth is the contribution of remittances by workers from the oil producing countries in the Middle East. The number of people who left Kafr el-Elow to work in the Persian Gulf and North African area is not known; however, their contribution to Kafr el-Elow is apparent.

With the expansion of housing, a new sewage system is being built for the first time in Kafr el-Elow. It is part of a larger sewage network for the greater Cairo metropolitan area which the Egyptian government is building with substantial economic aid from the U.S. government (AID). The cost of such a huge project has been estimated at L.E 3-4 billion. The impact of American foreign aid to this project was reflected in a remark made by the principal of the elementary school in Kafr el-Elow who stated that the Russians are known in Egypt for their help in building the Aswan Dam, and the Americans will be known for their contribution in building the sewage system for the greater Cairo area and maybe for the nation as a whole.

New public facilities have also been built in Kafr el-Elow during the previous two decades. Two new schools were built during the 1970's, an elementary and a junior high school. A new day-care center and pre-school nursery were built to provide services previously unavailable in the community, In addition, a vocational center for young girls to teach sewing and other handcraft skills was also built. A new post office was established from which the mail is distributed to people's homes by letter carriers. A garbage collection and street cleaning unit were established in the community. Eight new mosques were built during the past two decades. One of these mosques provides social services, health care, and religious education to the community. The cost of such services is supported by private donation and managed by organized religious groups.

The physical expansion and the changes which have taken place in the material component of Kafr el-Elow's culture during the past two decades have also affected the non-material component of their culture.

## Occupation and Mobility

The occupational structure has changed from essentially an agricultural one to one that is primarily industrial and commercial, thus requiring skilled

*Sign reflecting American AID project and participation in the construction of the greater Cairo sewage system.*

*Commercial outlets.*

and unskilled employment in addition to white-collar occupations. The increase in educational attainment has also created a new, but small, professional group. This trend reflects a new pattern of social mobility which creates basic changes in the community's social structure.

Industry is the largest employment source for the largest segment of the population in Kafr el-Elow. All of the big industrial firms in the area and most of the small ones are part of the public sector (*qitaa aam*), which is a government-owned and -managed operation. The employment policies of these industrial firms follow national government policies of employment. Employees, when hired, are assured of steady employment and entitled to all fringe benefits such as health insurance and a retirement pension. The average monthly salary, depending on the type of job and the skill of workers in industry, varies from L.E 100 to L.E 400 per month; however, the overall earnings of industrial workers tend to be higher than the average salary for civil servants. Based on the response of a survey conducted in Kafr el-Elow, 91 percent of all households have at least one member of their family employed by the surrounding industries. The new technological order created more jobs for the many who acquired skills which gave them more flexibility in terms of job selection and higher social and economic mobility. Furthermore, there has been an increase in the participation of females in industrial occupations and white-collar jobs.

Another source of employment for the people in Kafr el-Elow is reflected in the rapid growth of the commercial sector, where people either work for themselves or other individuals. This expansion of small individual commercial and industrial outlets continues to increase. In 1966, there were a total of 76 business units; in 1986, the number increased to 283 units. This represents a four-fold gain of commercial outlets during the past two decades. Many of these commercial outlets reflect the expansion of skilled employment which was still limited prior to 1966. There are many mechanical shops which provide services for vehicles of all types, especially trucks. In addition to providing electrical, welding, painting and pumping services, outlets also sell material for construction or produce tile sinks and bathroom products. The outlets which provide a broad variety of food, such as groceries, bakeries, butcher shops, coffee shops and restaurants, increased dramatically. The continuation of expansion and investment in the commercial sector in Kafr el-Elow shows the growing spirit of economic competition among the people of that community and also reveals that newcomers have settled in the area for economic gain.

The impact of the commercial sector, especially on the younger generation, is clear. The employment of young people of all ages is visible in the majority of these business outlets, especially that of young boys 7 to 16 years old. This is a new phenomenon which did not exist in Kafr el-Elow prior to 1966, but which prevailed in other urban areas in Egypt. The young boys are placed by their families in these workshops as apprentices under the supervision of the *osta* (a master skilled apprentice) to learn a skill. The earnings of these young boys during their apprenticeship vary from 20 to 30 piasters per day.[12] These boys are required to do certain jobs, under the supervision of the *osta*. The beginners are

---

[12]One Egyptian pound (L.E) is the equivalent of one hundred piasters.

*Distributor of soft drinks.*

*Young boy working in mechanical and tire repair shop.*

*Young boys working in mechanical and tire repair shop.*

referred to as *subyan* (boys), and they usually perform menial tasks, such as cleaning and handing tools to the *osta*. They learn the skill through observation. As soon as the youngster acquires the basic skill, he is referred to as *sanayi* (skilled worker). The new classification will also increase his earnings. The average daily earnings vary from L.E 4-L.E 8 per day.

Several factors contribute to the placement of these youngsters in workshops, despite the fact that law prohibits the employment of minors. Many of these youngsters come from poor families. The economic hardship, the impact of inflation, and the increase in the cost of living force many families to place their children in workshops to learn a trade and help the parents cope with their economic burden. The second factor which contributes to this situation is the lack of space in schools; therefore, the placement of children in such workshops is an appealing alternative to letting them roam the streets with nothing to do. Moreover, those who fail in school or perform poorly leave and are placed in such workshops to learn a skill and earn a living. The third rationale given is the future potential high earning of these youngsters after they learn a skill. Despite the fact that many of their parents emphasize the value of education, they are quick to point out that skilled workers earn more than a college graduate these days. Such consistency in the responses of some of these parents reflects a change in the values and attitudes of people in Kafr el-Elow.

## Education

Educational facilities have expanded and increasing numbers of children attend schools. Two new schools were built: an elementary school and a junior high school. The elementary school operates on a three-shift basis. The morning

*The new elementary and junior high schools.*

*The cement factory adjacent to the school playground.*

shift starts at 7:00 a.m.; the mid-day shift starts at 10:20 a.m.; and the afternoon shift starts at 2:00 p.m. The enrollment in each shift varies from 700-720 students. The total enrollment of both elementary schools reaches around 2,800 students.[13]

The junior high school operates on a two-shift basis. The first one starts at 7:00 and the second shift at 12:30 p.m. The total enrollment in the junior high is around 1400 students. All of the students enrolled in these schools are from Kafr el-Elow. The principals of both schools pointed out that the number of students would be higher if more space were available. According to government estimates, nearly 20 percent of children who reach school age nationwide are not admitted every year due to the lack of space.[14] Many of those students who finish the junior high school attend high schools in Helwan. The number of students attending institutions of higher learning has been increasing steadily. More than a hundred persons have already graduated from universities during the past two decades and more than that number are enrolled at various institutions of higher learning. People in Kafr el-Elow gradually dropped their opposition to the education of their girls. The remarkable rise in the educational attainment level of the younger generation creates increasing intergenerational mobility and discontinues traditional types of occupations. Nevertheless, Kafr el-Elow's illiteracy rate is still high. Nearly 45 percent of the population in that community still cannot read or write; this rate is consistent with the national average.

### The New Mass Media

A survey of two hundred homes in Kafr el-Elow revealed that 98 percent of the families own a television set and, in some cases, also a video set. This reflects a drastic change from the figures in 1966, when only six televisions were available in Kafr el-Elow. The proliferation of televisions in the 1980's resembles that of transistor radios in the 1960's; however, television has had a far greater impact. This influential medium has contributed in a significant way to cultural change in the local community, as well as in the nation at large. Television is now the main source of family entertainment. Through television, the people are not only exposed to the urban way of life, but also are thrust into the global setting through various foreign programs aired on the Egyptian national television network. For example, during the summer of 1986, the world soccer championship games which were held in Mexico City were shown simultaneously via satellite on Egyptian television nationwide. This medium has dismantled many of the traditional barriers between the urban and the rural settings.

This medium has expanded people's horizons beyond the boundaries of their community and their national state. The television network has also been used for private commercial advertisements since the beginning of the open-door economic policy. The ads generally focus and encourage consumption, which the nation needs the least. Furthermore, television influences and alters traditional patterns of social interaction within the community. The impact of

[13]All of the statistics used were obtained from school records in Kafr el-Elow.
[14]For further information see: *Al-ahram Iktisadi,* No. 799 (Cairo: 1984) [in Arabic].

television on people and their way of life has been significant; however, no research has been done in Egypt (as of 1986) to assess the extent of such impact.

Another medium which reflects the changes which have taken place in Kafr el-Elow during the past two decades is the availability of newspapers and magazines. There are now two outlets that sell newspapers and magazines in Kafr el-Elow. The availability of such types of mass media in addition to television and radio is destined to spread more political and social awareness among the people in Kafr el-Elow.

## Family and Kinship Organization

Familial and kinship organization reflects some changes and modification in functions as a result of its adaptation to the new economic and social order. After getting married, some of the younger generation, especially the educated ones, have started leaving their family households to establish their own nuclear families in separate residential units. The new location is determined by the availability of special accommodations. The majority of such cases were located in Kafr el-Elow and, in some cases, people moved to nearby communities.

One of the factors which encourages this trend is the increase in the exogamous marriage patterns among the younger generation. Many of the young people not only question the traditional endogamy marriage system and the choice of their parents, but also reject the traditional way by marrying outside their kin groups and choosing brides from other communities. The traditional arranged marriage pattern is being challenged by the younger generation. The new trend also affects the female segment of the community. where some are beginning to object and even reject their parents' choice of grooms; however, parents' responses to their offspring's wishes in general have been positive. Parents feel they have to adapt to their children's wishes and respect their individual rights of self-determination. In some cases, where the proposed marriage is not desirable, the parents only advise their children against it, but, in most cases, the children are the ones who will make the final decision. Many of the younger generation, especially those who are literate and employed, are in a better position socially and economically within their households. This situation enables them to influence decisions and directions. This trend implies that the lines of authority within the household are being challenged by the younger generation. This challenge, however, is not threatening the basic structure of the extended family. New roles are being acquired by the younger generation. An educated or a literate young person will be more persuasive with his illiterate parents. The old slogan that "parents know best" is being reversed to "young people know best." Nevertheless, parents, uncles, aunts, and grandparents are still respected and revered by the younger generation, although the elderly are no longer looked upon as the sole source of knowledge and experience by the literate young. The impact of modernization has contributed to the discontinuation of many of the traditional roles which the elderly used to perform in regard to the young.

.Another trend reflecting a decline in some of the basic functions of the family, especially in its economic functions, is that the family no longer produces some of its basic food needs as in the past. The family has changed from a producing into a consuming unit; now it depends on outside commercial outlets for its basic food needs. For example, the baking of bread used to be a weekly home task, but is no longer so. People now buy their bread from the bakeries in Kafr el-Elow at less cost, because it is subsidized by the government. The low price of bread encourages some people to buy more of it and even use it on a daily basis as a feed for their poultry or animals.

The day-care center provides for more than three hundred children between the ages of three and six years in Kafr el-Elow. The family used to be the main institution responsible for shaping the character and the personality of youngsters, especially during the formative years. Now, the nursery school and the day-care center, which was established six years ago, are contributing to this process for the first time in the history of that community. The day-care center is also providing new opportunities for married females with children to work outside their homes. More than half of the children in the day-care center have working mothers. Since the number of employed women with young children is still small, it would be premature to assess the impact of such employment on family life. Nevertheless, the employment of females also reflects a shift in role performance. Many of the young females with high school education are employed or seeking employment. Traditionally, the employment of females outside their own homes was not popular or supported by the family. Few were employed during the 1960's. Young men at the present time prefer to marry a girl who is employed over one who is not. The employment of the wife among the younger generation is viewed as a second source of income enabling the young family to cope with the high cost of living.

The increase in the cost of living, among other factors, has been responsible for some of the changes which have taken place among the younger generation. Modernization and changes in expectations for married life have altered many of the traditional customs and values associated with marriage. For example, there has been a substantial change in the amount of *mahr* (dowry) paid to the bride's family. The *mahr* increased from a few hundred Egyptian pounds on the average during the 1960's to a few thousand pounds during the 1980's. This increase is attributed to the changes in expectations, modernity, and the new lifestyle as defined by young people. When the average young girl gets married, she expects to have the basic home appliances such as a refrigerator, cooking stove, and washing machine, in addition to a bedroom set and dining and living room furniture.

There have also been some modifications in role performances within the household. The employment of unmarried girls might lessen their expectation of helping their mothers, but it will not relieve them completely of their domestic responsibilities. The girls continue to play subordinate roles to their parents. The father is still viewed as the head of the household and the breadwinner. He continues to be the dominant figure and center of authority and attention within the household. The sons continue to play roles subordinate to their fathers. If they are single and working, their roles are economically complementary to their fathers'. They contribute to the economic welfare of the family and are expected to save money for the dowry they must have when they decide to get married.

*New day-care center.*

*The youth athletic club and girls' vocational training center.*

The son's role and influence in family affairs tend to increase, especially if he is educated and is the main economic supporter of his family. Girls still play a subordinate role to their brothers. If a girl is more educated than her brother and employed, she would have more leverage in her relationship with her brother; however, education and employment will not give a girl complete freedom of movement within her family. The conjugal family in Kafr el-Elow remains in good shape and continues to provide many basic and essential services to its members.

Despite some of the changes which have occurred, the young people still subscribe to other norms and values of the extended family and have not abandoned their obligation and affiliation to their kinship group. Socialization between members of the extended family and their kin continues to take place. The frequency, however, of the social contact has decreased. The *mandara* (guest house), which used to be open in the evening for the members of the kin group to meet and interact with each other, has been discontinued. The use of the guest house is limited to social occasions such as deaths, weddings, holiday festivities, and special occasions. When people were asked about the causes of such change, they responded by saying, "people these days are busy and preoccupied with other essential things and do not have the spare time as they used to."

I will venture to say that the availability of TV sets in many homes contributed to this change. People prefer to stay home and watch television; however, loyalty to the family and the kinship network continues to have precedence over loyalty to the nation.

## Religion

Religiosity has increased since 1966, as is evident elsewhere in the nation. Eight new mosques have been built during the past two decades. The construction of these mosques was funded by private individuals and religious organizations such as the Ibrahimiya Sufi order.[15] Some of these new mosques are also used to provide some religious and social services. For example, the traditional religious education continues to be provided to youngsters who are taught to read, write, and memorize the Koran. The appeal of this type of education to parents in Kafr el-Elow did not diminish, but increased. Some of the children who attend the *Kuttab* consist of those who were not admitted to regular schools in Kafr el-Elow due to the lack of space. Other children who attend the *Kuttab* are the ones who combine religious education with the regular secular one. Since schools are run on a three-shift basis during the basic education period (elementary school) and the time spent at such schools is no more than three hours per day, students are still left with plenty of free time, a factor which encourages some of the parents to send their children to the *Kuttab* for religious education.

[15]Sufi orders are Islamic mystical religious brotherhood groups with an established social structure which embraces a very broad range of popular rituals and beliefs. Sufi orders are found in many Islamic countries. For further information on Sufism see: Spencer Trimingham, *The Sufi Orders in Islam* (Oxford: Oxford University Press, 1971).

The increase in religiosity in Kafr el-Elow is also reflected in the emphasis on observances of religious duties. For example, daily prayer, which used to be observed at home by many people, has shifted to the mosques. The observance of the Friday noon collective prayer by large numbers of people in all of the mosques in Kafr el-Elow is a clear and strong evidence of the increase in religiosity in that community, as it is in the nation as a whole. Religious observances, especially on the part of the young people has increased. It is not unusual to see young, ten-year-old boys joining the adults for the Friday noon sermon. Microphones and loudspeakers now replace the traditional call for prayer by the *muazen*.

The rise and establishment of branches of several Sufi religious orders in Kafr el-Elow also indicates increased religiosity. Most of the members of these Sufi orders are recruited from factories and other business establishments in the area. The rise of organized Islamic fundamental militant groups, especially among the young people in Kafr el-Elow, is a recent phenomenon. The Islamic fundamentalist movement is sweeping across the Middle East. It is posing a major political threat to the present regime in Egypt.[16] The number of people who belong to various Islamic fundamentalist groups in Kafr el-Elow is not known, but the observance of some physical signs reflects their presence: the wearing of a beard, the skullcap and the galabia, and a traditional flowing white gown are potent political symbols.

I met several people whom I was told by my informants belong to various Islamic organizations, but none of them were willing to be interviewed. A young university student, who is a member of one of the Islamic militant groups in Kafr el-Elow, told me if I want to seek information on their activities in the community, I should read the sign which they hung on the wall of a new building which was under construction at the time. The sign read the following: "The Islamic Center in Kafr el-Elow — The Committee for the Support of the Prophet's Tradition, (*As-sunnaal-muhamadiyya*)."[17]

The center consists of the following: a mosque, religious institute to train missionaries *(duaa)*, Islamic day-care center, Islamic library, student services and private, free tutoring, vocational training, and a free medical clinic.

Some of these services are already operational and the rest will be provided upon the completion of the construction. Similar services are provided by various militant Islamic groups all over Egypt. It is a very effective approach which provides them with grass-root support from people of various social and economic backgrounds.

During a discussion which I had with a highly respected religious leader in Kafr el-Elow, who is also a graduate of Al-azhar University, about the activities of the various Islamic militant movements, it was stated that they are committed to their cause and that their approach to the public through the free services they offer tends to be very effective and appealing. He further pointed out that the various Islamic militant groups are using Islam to promote their

---

[16]For further information on Islamic fundamentalist movements see: Nemat Guenena, "The Jihad: An Islamic Alternative in Egypt," *Cairo Papers in Social Science*, Vol. 9, (Summer 1986) [Cairo: American University in Cairo Press].

[17]*As-sunnas al-muhamadiyya* refers to the prophet's deeds and behavior.

*The new Ibrahimia mosque built by the Ibrahimia Sufi order.*

*New Mosque built by private donation.*

political cause. In addition, their interpretation of Islamic beliefs is not factual and far from the truth. Islamic fundamentalists have been viewed as a threat by the government. The frequent crackdowns by the government have not succeeded in suppressing the fundamentalists. Many of their leaders were sent to prison, especially after the assassination of President Sadat in October 1981. During the time I was in the field in 1986, 75 members were arrested in Cairo and were charged with setting fire to video tape rental shops, a movie theatre, and a grocery store selling alcohol in Cairo. The number of video tape shops and organized video clubs has been increasing nationwide, due to the increase in the sales of video machines since the early 1980's. Some of the video tapes sold to the public are smuggled into Egypt from abroad and their contents tend to be incompatible with that society's norms and values. To the religious fanatic, such commercial outlets represent a threat to Islamic teachings and society's moral order, and, therefore, should be eliminated. Also, the consumption of alcohol is prohibited according to Islam, and should not be sold to the public. During the past few years, several attempts were made by members of the People's Assembly *(majliss il-shaab)* to pass a law prohibiting the sale of alcoholic beverages in Egypt. Such an attempt was not successful.

None of the commercial outlets in Kafr el-Elow sell alcoholic beverages. During the early 1960's, only two food outlets in Kafr el-Elow sold beer on a very small scale to a few young people who used to consume it in secrecy. The elimination of such activities reflected the impact and influence of religiosity in Kafr el-Elow, which is again consistent with the national trend.

Another factor which also reflects the increase in religiosity is the increasing number of people who go on pilgrimages to Mecca. The lifting of travel restrictions by the government and the improvement of the economic conditions of people in Kafr el-Elow have contributed to this increase.

Popular beliefs and practices associated with Islam such as the evil eye, the cult of charms, and the zar cult continue to thrive. The observances and celebration of religious festivities and holidays by the people in Kafr el-Elow continue. More emphasis is placed on fasting during the month of Ramadan by the adult population; however, the traditional collective rituals which used to be observed during the month of Ramadan have been modified. For example, the male members of the clan no longer meet in their *mandara* (guest house) during the month of Ramadan to eat the *iftar* meal together. Even the traditional gathering for the reading of the Koran and hearing the *tarawih* (religious chantings) at the guest house have been discontinued. In general, people stay home and watch TV, which usually provides special programs during the month of Ramadan. The video set, which many people now possess, also adds to the entertainment variety for the members of the household; those who want to hear a Koran recitation can do so by using the video.[18]

## Conclusion

From the preceding accounts, it is clear that the expansion and growth of industrialization, urbanization and the development of small-scale enterprises in

[18]Religious video tapes are available and sold by commercial outlets all over Egypt.

the area have expedited the process of cultural change in Kafr el-Elow. It is also obvious that economic gain has been the most influential factor fostering changes at all levels. It has produced a relative affluence for the average person in the community which, in return, has contributed to a change in the conditions of their daily life. The rapid changes which took place, especially in the occupational structure, occurred with eagerness and rapid swiftness. The average occupational level of Kafr el-Elow's families improved in many gratifying ways during the past two decades. Many of the traditional occupations, such as agricultural work, have been eliminated completely among the younger generation, and the adaptation has been accomplished smoothly.

The economic gains achieved by the people in Kafr el-Elow have influenced the traditional social structure, and have also contributed to the expansion of their daily personal contact with outsiders. This trend has influenced and has permitted the rise of new groups within the community, which in return has influenced the social network and group interaction. For example, social interaction with non-relatives has increased. This also has influenced and has modified the scope and functions of kinship ties; however, affiliation with and support for the kin group did not diminish. Personalized relations among the members of the kinship group still predominate and appear to be an essential ingredient in the maintenance of the kinship network. The notion that the impact of urbanization and industrialization will contribute to the disintegration of the extended family and of the kinship system did not appear in Kafr el-Elow, and I doubt that it will appear in the foreseeable future. Furthermore, the social problems associated with urban industrial life have not occurred in this community. For example, there has been neither an increase in family instability, nor in the divorce rate. The problems of crime and juvenile delinquency are unheard of and will not be tolerated. One of the major factors contributing to this situation is the economic well-being shared by the people in Kafr el-Elow. Also, the stability of the family and strength of kinship ties among the members of kin groups and the impact of religiosity contribute to the stability of the community. The increase in secularization has not lessened the influence of religion on the people of Kafr el-Elow. The level of religious beliefs and participation has not only continued, but increased in intensity; its sway is stronger in 1986 than it was in the 1960's. The people of Kafr el-Elow continue to experience and adjust to the winds of enormous economic and social forces; yet, they hold on fiercely to many of their social values. On the other hand, some of the main difficulties which confront the people in Kafr el-Elow in general are environmental air and water pollution, brought about by urban industrial life. The congestion, the cramped living space, and the hazards of traffic are also a source of tension and irritation to many people in the community. These problems are not unique to Kafr el-Elow, but apply also to the nation at large.

# Glossary

*abou:* father
*adala:* justice
*ahl:* relatives
*aila* (pl. *ailaat*): joint family
*ain:* eye
*ain il-hasud:* the evil eye
*aish:* bread
*ajr:* good deeds
*akh:* brother
*akhwal* (sing. *khal*): maternal uncle
*ala:* on
*al-hajj:* pilgrimage
*al-hayy-al-gayyum:* who is living and present everywhere
*alkabeer:* the big
*al-tawheed Lil-lah:* God, he is the one
*amm* (pl. *amam*): paternal uncle
*ammeh:* paternal aunt
*amoud el-bait:* pillar of the house
*anker:* a big brass dish
*aras:* sant tree
*arees:* groom
*arkan al-din:* foundation of religion
*arusa:* bride
*As-Sunna:* the prophet tradition and conduct
*ash-shehada:* testimony, to profess faith
*aslama:* submission
*asr:* afternoon
*as-salat:* prayer
*assaum:* fast
*awlad* (sing. *walad*): boys
*azaa:* mourning
*az-zakat:* almsgiving
*badla:* suit
*bait:* house
*baladi:* local, rural
*ballana:* a village woman who beautifies brides for their weddings
*bint* (pl. *banat*): girl
CLAN: A group of persons who believe themselves linked by common descent. In the village membership is traced through the father's side and it is an overgrown lineage—more than five or six generations. The use of the term "clan" varies greatly among anthropologists.
COLLATERAL GENERATION: Consanguine relatives not directly connected by descent to the next generation.

*daar:* house
*dafin:* burial
*dakka:* beat
*dariba:* taxes collected by the government
*daya:* mid-wife
*diyya:* blood money
*elow:* height
ENDOGAMY: The practice of a person seeking a mate within his group. In the village there are no rules against marrying outsiders; however, it is not the preferred practice.
EXTENDED FAMILY: A family consisting of a series of close relatives along the male line. A father, his wife, their children and their married sons with their wives. Also unmarried paternal aunts and married and unmarried uncles.
*farah:* joy
*fatiha:* the opening chapter of the Koran
*fatir:* pastries
*fatwa:* formal legal opinion
*feddan:* acre
*fellaheen* (sing. *fellah*): peasants, farmers
*fellahi:* adjective form of fellah: peasant
*firdaus:* paradise
*forat id-dam:* the boiling of the blood
*fuul:* fava beans
*galla:* dung
*gamousa:* water buffalo
*garafa:* cemetery
*gazzar:* butcher
*gezira:* island
*ghafeer:* guard
*ghagarieh:* gypsy
*ghurza:* coffee house
*goza:* water pipe
*hadith: lit.* "talk"; sayings attributed to prophet Muhammad
*hagg:* just, right
*hajji* (fem. *hajjeh*): a person who performs the pilgrimage
*hama:* father-in-law
*hammah:* mother-in-law
*hamula:* clan
*henna:* henna
*haram:* forbidden
*hardana:* a wife who returns to her parents' home following an argument with her husband
*hareem:* females
*harrath:* the one who ploughs the land
*hasanah* (pl. *hasanat*): good deeds
*haush:* courtyard, household
*hejab:* charms to protect bearer from the evil eye
*hidad:* mourning
*hokouk al walidain:* the parents' rights
*houssa:* share
*hurriya:* freedom
*ibn:* son
*iftar:* the meal to break fasting
*il-istimar:* imperialism
*ilqwmiya:* nationalism

*il-tarawih:* religious songs
*in sha Allah: lit.* "if God wills it"
*isha:* evening
*ishtirakiya:* socialism
*Itihad il-arabi il-ishtiraki: lit.* "Arab Socialist Union Party"
*jabbanah:* cemetery
*jalabiya:* garb
*jidd* (fem. *jidah*): grandfather
JOINT FAMILY: Several related families in one household, usually parents and their
    children (married sons and their families residing in a common residence).
*kabeer il-aila:* the elder of the family
*kabir:* large, great
*kafan:* grave clothes
*kafeel:* co-signer
*kafr:* clustering of people
*kahik:* cookies
*kahwa:* coffee
*karaamat: lit.* "good deeds"
*karam:* generosity
*kareem:* generous
*kash:* straw, hay
*katib il-kitab: lit.* "engagement," ritual of signing the marriage contract
*kghafara allah thanbakum: lit.* "May God forgive your sins"
*khal* (fem. *khalah*): maternal uncle
*khawajat* (sing. *khawaja*): foreigners
*Khelow:* key money
*khoum:* chicken coop
*khoutba:* sermon
*khumss:* one fifth
*kism:* subadministrative unit
*kismah wa nasseeb: lit.* "luck"
*kohl:* kohl, eye makeup
*lagnat:* committee
*lailat:* night, evening
*lailat iddukhla:* wedding night
LEVIRATE MARRIAGE: The practice which permits a man to marry the widow of his
    brother.
LINEAGE: A group of persons linked together through traceable descent to a common
    ancestor reckoned exclusively through one sex. Arabs reckon this descent through
    the father. Membership in a lineage allocates special rituals, rights, and obligations
    to persons and things in the community.
*maghrib:* evening
*mahkama il-sharia:* a Muslim canon court
*mahr:* bride price
*majliss:* council
*makan:* place
*mandara:* guest house, hospitality house in the village
*markaz:* police station
*Ma-Sha-Allah: lit.* "The power of God is so great"
*masrahiah:* stage play
*matraha:* flat wooden plate
*maujoud:* present
*mayyet:* dead
*mazun:* marriage registrar
*mirat:* wife

*mouhafaza:* governorate
*mouhafiz:* governor
*moukhabarat:* secret police, communication
*mouzayin:* barber
*muakhar:* delayed
*muassal:* sweet tobacco
*Muazen:* the caller for prayer
*mufti:* religious judge
*mugaddam:* in advance
*mughassil:* washer of the dead
*mujid or mukre:* the one who recites from the Koran on special occasions such as mourning
*mulk:* private property
*munat il-bait:* basic food for house consumption
*musahir:* village crier
*musharaka:* partnership
*muttahir:* itinerant who performs circumcisions
*nabi:* prophet
*nadar:* vow
*nadi:* club
*nafaka:* alimony
*nkout:* gift
NUCLEAR FAMILY: A married couple with their children.
*omda:* village head
*Osta:* master skilled apprentice
PARALLEL-COUSIN MARRIAGE: Marriage between cousins related through the siblings of the same sex (e.g., in the village it is the marriage between the child of a man and the child of his brother).
PATERNAL: Relationships associated with the father (it is the opposite of maternal).
PATRILINEAL DESCENT: The transmission of name and authority through males.
PATRILOCAL: Residential pattern whereby the wife lives with her husband's family.
POLYGYNY: A form of marriage in which a man may have more than one wife at the same time (Islam permits four wives at a time).
*qibla:* eastward
*qitaa-amm:* public sector
*rab al aila: lit.* "master of the house"
*raheem:* merciful
*rejalla:* men
*riadi:* athletic
*rizka and/or sutra: lit.* "livelihood"; the amount paid to a judge under customary law by the party found in the wrong
*rouhi talka: lit.* "you are divorced"
*sadagaat:* good deeds
*sahra:* evening gathering, evening entertainment
*sahur:* meal eaten before resumption of the fast
*salam:* peace
*salat al-asr:* afternoon prayer
*salat al-magrib:* evening prayer
*salat al-thur:* noon prayer
*salat es-subh:* morning prayer
*Sanayi:* skilled worker
*sarraf:* tax collector
*sewan:* tent
*shabab* (sing. *shab*): youth
*shahim* (adj. *shahama*): generous

*shaik* (pl. *shuyuk*): head of a clan
*shakara:* to express thanks and appreciation
*sharaf:* honor
*sharbat:* soft drinks
*sharia:* Islamic canon law
*shirk:* polytheism
SORORAL POLYGYNY: A form of marriage in which one man marries several sisters.
*Subyan:* plural of *sabi*-boy
*sulha:* a peace ceremony
*suq:* market
*tabla:* drum
*tahuur:* circumcision
*tari:* soft
*tariqa:* religious brotherhood
*tarzi:* tailor
*tesht:* large dish
*thar:* revenge
*torat id dam:* the boiling of the blood
*tura:* canal
*ukht:* sister
*umm:* mother
*urf law:* customary law
*wahid: lit.* "indivisible"
*waqf:* endowment to a religious institution
*waseet:* mediator
*wasfat baladiya:* folk medicine
*yamin:* oath
*youm addukhla:* wedding day
*youm el-shabka:* engagement day
*zaffah:* a wedding procession
*zagareet:* women's cry of joy
*zareeba:* barn, shelter for animals
*zeer:* pottery jar
*ziyara: lit.* "visit"; a special festival
*zoug:* husband
*zougit:* wife

# References

ABOU ZAID, A., 1963, "Vendetta: An Anthropological Study in an Upper Egyptian Village," *The National Review of Criminal Science*, Vol. 6, No. 3, pp. 301–364.

AMMAR, HAMAD, 1966, *Growing Up in an Egyptian Village*. New York: Octagon Books.

AYOUB, VICTOR, 1964, "Conflict Resolution and Social Reorganization in a Lebanese Village," *Human Organization*, Vol. 24, No. 1, pp. 11–18.

AYROUT, HABIB, 1963, *The Egyptian Peasant*. Boston: Beacon Press.

BARCLAY, HAROLD, 1964, *Buurri al Lamaab: A Suburban Village in the Sudan*. Ithaca: Cornell University Press.

BEHMAN, FRANCINE, 1953 "The Zar Cult in Egypt." Cairo: The American University in Cairo (master's thesis).

BERGER, MORROE, 1962, *The Arab World Today*. New York: Doubleday and Co.

BUBRESS, D., 1966 "Muthalath Al-Raab," *Al-Mussawar Journal*, No. 2197, pp. 7–12, (in Arabic).

DAWOOD, J. N. (trans.), 1959, *The Koran*. Harmondsworth, England: Penguin Books Ltd.

EVANS-PRITCHARD, E. E., 1949, *The Sanusi of Cyrenaica*. Oxford: Oxford University Press.

FIRTH, R., 1964, "Family and Kinship in Industrial Society," *Sociological Review*, Monograph no. 8, Keele.

GRUNEBAUM, GUSTAVE E., VON, 1953, *Medieval Islam: A Study in Cultural Orientation*. Chicago: University of Chicago Press.

GULICK, JOHN, 1955, *Social Structure and Culture Change in a Lebanese Village*. New York: Wenner-Gren Foundation.

HAMADY, S., 1960, *Temperament and Character of the Arabs*. New York: Twayne Publishers.

HARDY, H., 1963, *Blood Feuds and the Payment of Blood Money in the Middle East*. Netherlands: Leiden Brill Co.

HIRABAYASHI, G., and KHATIB, M., 1958, "Communication and Political Awareness in the Villages of Egypt," *Public Opinion Quarterly*, Vol. 22, pp. 357–363.

KERR, MALCOLM, 1962, "The Emergence of a Socialist Ideology in Egypt," *The Middle East Journal*, Vol. 16, No. 2, pp. 127–144.

LERNER, DANIEL, 1958, *The Passing of Traditional Society: Modernizing the Middle East*. Glencoe, Ill.: The Free Press.

LUTFIYYA, A., 1966, *Baytin: A Jordanian Village*. The Hague: Mouton and Co.

MEAD, MARGARET, 1954, *Cultural Patterns and Technical Change*. New York: UNESCO Publication.

MURPHY, R., and KASDAN, L., 1959, "The Structure of Parallel Cousin Marriage," *American Anthropologist*, Vol. 61, pp. 17–29.

PICKTHALL, MARMADUKE (trans.), 1952, *The Meaning of the Glorious Koran: An Explanatory Translation*. London: George Allen & Unwin, Ltd.

REDFIELD, ROBERT, 1961, *The Little Community—Peasant Society and Culture.* Chicago: University of Chicago Press.

SINGER, M., and COHN, B. (eds.), 1968, *Structure and Change in Indian Society.* New York: Wenner-Gren Foundation.

*U.A.R. Census Book, 1917, 1937, 1947, 1960.* Cairo, U.A.R.

WATSON, WILLIAM, 1958, *Tribal Cohesion in a Money Economy.* Manchester: Manchester University Press.

# Recommended Reading

ADAMS, RICHARD, 1986, *Development and Social Change in Rural Egypt*. Syracuse: Syracuse University Press.

ANSARI, HAMIED, 1986, *Egypt, The Stalled Society*. Albany, NY: State University of New York Press.

ASAD, TALAL and ROGER OWEN, (eds.), 1983, *Sociology of Developing Societies: The Middle East*. New York: Monthly Review Press.

BURNS, WILLIAM J., 1985, *Economic Aid and American Policy Toward Egypt, 1955-1981*. Albany, NY: State University of New York Press.

GILSENAN, MICHAEL, 1982, *Recognizing Islam: Religion and Society in the Modern Arab World*. New York: Pantheon Books.

GUENENA, NEMAT, 1986, "The 'Jihad': An Islamic Alternative in Egypt," *Cairo Papers in Social Science*, Vol. 9. Cairo: American University in Cairo Press.

IBRAHIM, SAAD EDDIN, and NICHOLAS HOPKINS (eds.), 1984, *Arab Society in Transition: A Reader*. Cairo: American University in Cairo Press.

IBRAHIM, SAAD EDDIN, 1982, *The New Arab Social Order: A Study of the Social Impact of Oil Wealth*. Boulder, CO: Westview Press, Inc.

KHURI, FUAD, 1975, *From Village to Suburb: Order and Change in Greater Beirut*, Chicago: University of Chicago Press.

MARTIN, RICHARD, 1982, *Islam*. Englewood Cliffs, NJ: Prentice-Hall, Inc.

MARSOT, AFAF LUTFI AL-SAYYID, 1985, *A Short History of Modern Egypt*. New York: Cambridge University Press.

WATERBURY, JOHN, 1983. *The Egypt of Nasser and Sadat: The Political Economy of Two Regimes*. Princeton, NJ: Princeton University Press.